MANHATTAN GMAT

Word Problems

GMAT Strategy Guide

This comprehensive guide analyzes the GMAT's complex word problems
and provides structured frameworks for attacking each question type. Master
the art of translating challenging word problems into organized data.

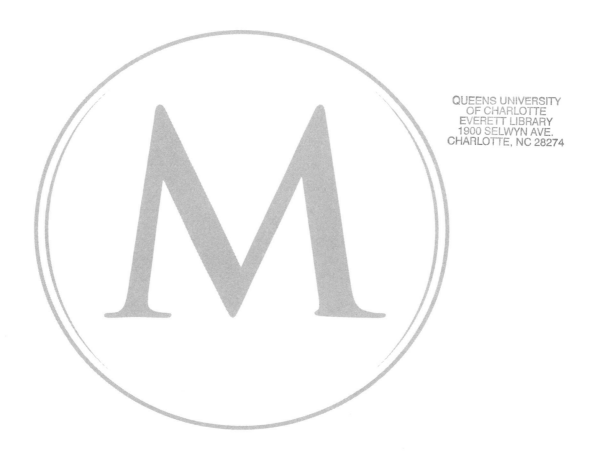

guide 3

MIX
Paper from
responsible sources

FSC
www.fsc.org

Word Problems GMAT Strategy Guide, Fifth Edition

10-digit International Standard Book Number: 1-935707-68-X
13-digit International Standard Book Number: 978-1-935707-68-4
eISBN: 978-1-937707-09-5

Copyright © 2012 MG Prep, Inc.

ALL RIGHTS RESERVED. No part of this work may be reproduced or used in any form or
by any means—graphic, electronic, or mechanical, including photocopying, recording,
taping, web distribution—without the prior written permission of the publisher,
MG Prep, Inc.

Note: *GMAT, Graduate Management Admission Test, Graduate Management Admission
Council,* and *GMAC* are all registered trademarks of the Graduate Management Admission
Council, which neither sponsors nor is affiliated in any way with this product.

Layout Design: Dan McNaney and Cathy Huang
Cover Design: Evyn Williams and Dan McNaney
Cover Photography: Alli Ugosoli

INSTRUCTIONAL GUIDE SERIES

SUPPLEMENTAL GUIDE SERIES

MANHATTAN
GMAT

April 24th, 2012

Dear Student,

Thank you for picking up a copy of *Word Problems*. I hope this book provides just the guidance you need to get the most out of your GMAT studies.

As with most accomplishments, there were many people involved in the creation of the book you are holding. First and foremost is Zeke Vanderhoek, the founder of Manhattan GMAT. Zeke was a lone tutor in New York when he started the company in 2000. Now, 12 years later, the company has instructors and offices nationwide and contributes to the studies and successes of thousands of students each year.

Our Manhattan GMAT Strategy Guides are based on the continuing experiences of our instructors and students. For this volume, we are particularly indebted to Dave Mahler and Stacey Koprince. Dave deserves special recognition for his contributions over the past number of years. Dan McNaney and Cathy Huang provided their design expertise to make the books as user-friendly as possible, and Noah Teitelbaum and Liz Krisher made sure all the moving pieces came together at just the right time. And there's Chris Ryan. Beyond providing additions and edits for this book, Chris continues to be the driving force behind all of our curriculum efforts. His leadership is invaluable. Finally, thank you to all of the Manhattan GMAT students who have provided input and feedback over the years. This book wouldn't be half of what it is without your voice.

At Manhattan GMAT, we continually aspire to provide the best instructors and resources possible. We hope that you will find our commitment manifest in this book. If you have any questions or comments, please email me at dgonzalez@manhattanprep.com. I'll look forward to reading your comments, and I'll be sure to pass them along to our curriculum team.

Thanks again, and best of luck preparing for the GMAT!

Sincerely,

Dan Gonzalez
President
Manhattan GMAT

HOW TO ACCESS YOUR ONLINE RESOURCES

If you...

⊙ **are a registered Manhattan GMAT student**

and have received this book as part of your course materials, you have AUTOMATIC access to ALL of our online resources. This includes all practice exams, question banks, and online updates to this book. To access these resources, follow the instructions in the Welcome Guide provided to you at the start of your program. Do NOT follow the instructions below.

⊙ **purchased this book from the Manhattan GMAT online store or at one of our centers**

1. Go to: www.manhattanprep.com/gmat/studentcenter.

2. Log in using the username and password used when your account was set up.

⊙ **purchased this book at a retail location**

1. Create an account with Manhattan GMAT at the website: www.manhattanprep.com/gmat/register.

2. Go to: www.manhattanprep.com/gmat/access.

3. Follow the instructions on the screen.

Your one year of online access begins on the day that you register your book at the above URL.

You only need to register your product ONCE at the above URL. To use your online resources any time AFTER you have completed the registration process, log in to the following URL: www.manhattanprep.com/gmat/studentcenter.

Please note that online access is nontransferable. This means that only NEW and UNREGISTERED copies of the book will grant you online access. Previously used books will NOT provide any online resources.

⊙ **purchased an eBook version of this book**

1. Create an account with Manhattan GMAT at the website: www.manhattanprep.com/gmat/register.

2. Email a copy of your purchase receipt to gmat@manhattanprep.com to activate your resources. Please be sure to use the same email address to create an account that you used to purchase the eBook.

For any technical issues, email techsupport@manhattanprep.com or call 800-576-4628.

Please refer to the following page for a description of the online resources that come with this book.

YOUR ONLINE RESOURCES

Your purchase includes ONLINE ACCESS to the following:

⊙ 6 Computer-Adaptive Online Practice Exams

The 6 full-length computer-adaptive practice exams included with the purchase of this book are delivered online using Manhattan GMAT's proprietary computer-adaptive test engine. The exams adapt to your ability level by drawing from a bank of more than 1,200 unique questions of varying difficulty levels written by Manhattan GMAT's expert instructors, all of whom have scored in the 99th percentile on the Official GMAT. At the end of each exam you will receive a score, an analysis of your results, and the opportunity to review detailed explanations for each question. You may choose to take the exams timed or untimed.

The content presented in this book is updated periodically to ensure that it reflects the GMAT's most current trends and is as accurate as possible. You may view any known errors or minor changes upon registering for online access.

Important Note: The 6 computer adaptive online exams included with the purchase of this book are the SAME exams that you receive upon purchasing ANY book in the Manhattan GMAT Complete Strategy Guide Set.

⊙ *Word Problems* Online Question Bank

The Bonus Online Question Bank for *Word Problems* consists of 25 extra practice questions (with detailed explanations) that test the variety of concepts and skills covered in this book. These questions provide you with extra practice beyond the problem sets contained in this book. You may use our online timer to practice your pacing by setting time limits for each question in the bank.

⊙ Online Updates to the Contents in this Book

The content presented in this book is updated periodically to ensure that it reflects the GMAT's most current trends. You may view all updates, including any known errors or changes, upon registering for online access.

TABLE *of* CONTENTS

Chapter 1
of
Word Problems

Algebraic Translations

In This Chapter...

Chapter 1:
Algebraic Translations

Word problems are prevalent on the GMAT, and it is important to develop a consistent process for answering them. Almost any word problem can be broken down into four steps:

1. Identify what value the question is asking for. We'll call this the **desired value**.
2. Identify **unknown values** and **label** them with **variables**.
3. Identify **relationships** and **translate** them into **equations**.
4. Use the equations to **solve** for the desired value.

In essence, you need to turn a word problem into a system of equations, and use those equations to solve for the desired value.

Answer the following question by following these four steps.

> A candy company sells premium chocolate at $5 per pound and regular chocolates at $4 per pound. If Barrett buys a 7-pound box of chocolates that costs him $31, how many pounds of premium chocolates are in the box?

Step 1: Identify the *desired value.*

The question asks for the number of pounds of premium chocolate that Barrett bought.

Once you have assigned variables to unknown values, you can express this question in terms of those variables.

Step 2: Identify *unknown values* and *label* them with *variables.*

Any quantity that you do not have a concrete value for qualifies as an unknown value.

Which quantities? Try to use as few variables as possible while still accounting for all the unknown values described in the question. The more variables you use, the more equations you will need.

1

In this question, there are two basic unknown values: the number of pounds of premium chocolate and the number of pounds of regular chocolate.

Which letters? Use descriptive letters. x and y, while classic choices, do not immediately tell whether x is premium and y is regular or vice versa. The following labels are more descriptive:

p = pounds of premium chocolate
r = pounds of regular chocolate

Never forget to include **units**! The units for these unknowns are pounds. Units can be a very helpful guide as relationships become more complicated. We'll discuss units in more detail later in the chapter.

This would be a good time to express the question in terms of p and r. If you write "$p = ?$" on your page, you have a quick reminder of the desired value (in case you lose track).

Step 3: Identify *relationships* and *translate* them into *equations*.

Which relationships? A good general principle is that you will need as many relationships (and hence equations) as unknown values. You have two unknown values, so you should expect two relationships that we can turn into equations.

One fairly straightforward relationship concerns the total number of pounds of chocolate. Barrett bought a 7-pound box of chocolate. If the box contains only regular and premium chocolate, then you can write the following equation:

$r + p = 7$

The other relationship concerns the total cost of the box. The total cost of the box is equal to the cost of the premium chocolates plus the cost of the regular chocolates.

This relationship is slightly more complicated than it appears, because it involves a relationship the GMAT expects you to know: *Total Cost = Unit Price × Quantity*. Just as you want to minimize the number of variables you create, you want to minimize the number of equations you have to create. You can express all three terms in the above equation using information you already have:

Total Cost of Box = \$31
Cost of Premiums = (5 \$/pound) × (p pounds) = $5p$
Cost of Regulars = (4 \$/pound) × (r pounds) = $4r$

Note that you can translate "dollars per pound" to "\$/pound." In general, the word "per" should be translated as "divided by."

Put that all together, and you have your second equation:

$31 = 5p + 4r$

Step 4: Use the equations to *solve* for the desired value.

These are the two equations you have to work with:

$$r + p = 7$$
$$31 = 5p + 4r$$

Remember that you need to find the value of p. Generally, the most efficient way to find the desired value is to *eliminate unwanted variables using substitution.*

If you eliminate r, you will be left with the variable p, which is the variable you are trying to solve for. To eliminate r, first isolate it in one of the equations. r is easier to isolate in the first equation:

$$r + p = 7 \qquad \rightarrow \qquad r = 7 - p$$

Now replace r with $(7 - p)$ in the second equation and solve for p:

$$31 = 5p + 4(7 - p)$$
$$31 = 5p + 28 - 4p$$
$$3 = p$$

The GMAT has many ways of making various stages of a word problem more difficult, which is why it is so important to have a good process. Train yourself to use these four steps to stay on track and continually work towards a solution.

Also note: these steps do not have to be followed in strict order. Rather, successfully completing a word problem means completing each step successfully *at some point* in the process.

Pay Attention to Units

Unlike problems that test pure algebra, word problems have a context. The values, both unknown and known, have a meaning. Practically, this means that every value in a word problem has units.

Every equation that correctly represents a relationship has units that make sense. Most relationships are either additive or multiplicative.

Additive Relationships

In the chocolates problem, there were two additive relationships:

$$r + p = 7$$
$$31 = 5p + 4r$$

1

The reason that each of these equations makes sense is that for each equation, **the units of every term are the same**. Also, **adding terms with the same units does not change the units**. Here are the same equations with the units added in parentheses:

r (pounds of chocolate) + p (pounds of chocolate) = 7 (pounds of chocolate)
31 (dollars) = 5p (dollars) + 4r (dollars)

You may be wondering how you can know the units for 5p and 4r are dollars. That brings us to the second type of relationship.

Multiplicative Relationships

Remember the relationship you used to find those two terms?

Total Cost = Unit Price × Quantity

Look at them again with units in parentheses:

$$5\left(\frac{\text{dollars}}{\text{pound}}\right) \times p \text{ (pounds)} = 5p \text{ (dollars)}$$

$$4\left(\frac{\text{dollars}}{\text{pound}}\right) \times r \text{ (pounds)} = 4r \text{ (dollars)}$$

For multiplicative relationships, **treat units like numerators and denominators**. Units that are multiplied together DO change.

In the equations above, pounds in the denominator of the first term cancel out pounds in the denominator of the second term, leaving dollars as the final units:

$$5\left(\frac{\text{dollars}}{\cancel{\text{pounds}}}\right) \times p \text{ (}\cancel{\text{pounds}}\text{)} = 5p \text{ (dollars)}$$

Look at the formula for area to see what happens to the same units when they appear on the same side of the fraction:

l (feet) × w (feet) = lw (feet^2)

Common Relationships

1

Although the GMAT requires little factual knowledge, it will assume that you have mastered the following relationships. Notice that for all of these relationships, the units follow the rules laid out in the last section:

- Total Cost ($) = Unit Price ($/unit) × Quantity Purchased (units)
- Profit ($) = Revenue ($) − Cost ($)
- Total Earnings ($) = Wage Rate ($/hour) × Hours Worked (hours)
- Miles = Miles per Hour × Hours
- Miles = Miles per Gallon × Gallons

Units Conversion

When values with units are multiplied or divided, the units change. This property is the basis of using **conversion factors** to convert units. A conversion factor is a fraction whose numerator and denominator have different units but the same value.

For instance, how many seconds are in 7 minutes? If you said 420, you'd be correct. You were able to make this calculation because you know there are 60 seconds in a minute. $\dfrac{60 \text{ seconds}}{1 \text{ minute}}$ is a conversion factor. Because the numerator and denominator are the same, multiplying by a conversion factor is just a sneaky way of multiplying by 1. The multiplication looks like this:

$$7 \text{ minutes} \times \frac{60 \text{ seconds}}{1 \text{ minute}} = 420 \text{ seconds}$$

Because you are multiplying, you can cancel minutes, leaving you with your desired units (seconds). Questions will occasionally center around your ability to convert units. Try the following example:

> A certain medicine requires 4 doses per day. If each dose is 150 milligrams, how many milligrams of medicine will a person have taken after the end of the third day, if the medicine is used as directed?

For any question that involves units conversion, there will have to be some concrete value given. In this case, you were told that the time period is three days.

Now you need to know what the question is asking for. It's asking for the number of milligrams of medicine that can be taken in that time. In other words, you need to change from days to milligrams.

The question has given you several conversion factors you can use. Four doses per day is one, and 150 milligrams per dose is the other. you can combine the calculations into one big expression:

1

$$3 \text{ days} \times \frac{4 \text{ doses}}{1 \text{ day}} \times \frac{150 \text{ milligrams}}{1 \text{ dose}} = 1,800 \text{ milligrams}$$

During the GMAT, you may not actually write out the units for each piece of multiplication. Even if you don't, however, make sure that you use conversion factors to cancel units in the numerator and denominator.

Integer Constraints

Some word problems will, by their nature, restrict the possible values of variables. The most common restriction is that variables must be integers. For instance, any variable that represents the number of cars, people, marbles, etc., must be an integer.

These restrictions are dangerous because they are so obvious. Take a look at the following Problem Solving problem:

> If Kelly received 1/3 more votes than Mike in a student election, which of the following could have been the total number of votes cast for the two candidates?
>
> (A) 54   (B) 55   (C) 56   (D) 57   (E) 58

The number of votes cast for each candidate must be a whole number. But how does that affect this question? To answer that, first answer the question, "Could Mike have received 1 vote?"

No, he could not have. If Kelly received 1/3 more votes than Mike, she received 4/3 the number of votes. If he received 1 vote, then Kelly received 1 × 4/3 = 4/3 votes. That doesn't make sense.

So what times 4/3 *will* equal an integer? Only multiples of 3 will cancel out the 3 in the denominator. So Mike must have received a number of votes that is a multiple of 3. See if you can figure out a pattern:

Mike	Kelly	Total
3	4	7
6	8	14
9	12	21

Do you see the pattern? If the number of votes Mike received is a multiple of 3, then the number of votes Kelly received must be a multiple of 4. Taken together, the total number of votes cast must then be a multiple of 7.

The only answer choice that is a multiple of 7 is (C) 56. Therefore, that is the correct answer. Without recognizing the integer constraint, you would not have been able to answer this question.

Hidden Constraints also show up on Data Sufficiency. (For an in-depth look at the Data Sufficiency problem type, refer to Chapter 6.) They work well with Data Sufficiency because information that seems like it should be insufficient on its own actually does provide an answer. Try the following example:

> A store sells erasers for $0.23 each and pencils for $0.11 each. How many erasers and pencils did Jessica buy from the store?
>
> (1) Jessica bought 5 erasers.
> (2) Jessica spent $1.70 on erasers and pencils.

Statement 1 by itself is definitely not sufficient. You have no information about the number of pencils Jessica bought. Cross off A and D.

On the surface, it also seems like Statement 2 should not be enough on its own. The clue that it may be is the weird prices of the two products: $0.23 and $0.11. Each of these values needs to be multiplied by an integer (because you cannot buy a fraction of a pencil), so it may be the case that there is only one way for a combination of pencils and erasers to cost $1.70.

Convert to cents to make the calculations easier. If Jessica bought 1 eraser, then she would have spent 170 – 23 = 147 cents on pencils. But 147 isn't divisible by 11. Keep testing numbers. 2 erasers cost 46 cents, but 124 isn't divisible by 11 either.

As it turns out, the only combination that works is 5 erasers and 5 pencils: $5 \times 23 + 5 \times 11 = 170$. Statement 2 is sufficient by itself. The correct answer is (B).

Always be aware of limitations placed upon variables. The most common limitation requires a variable to be an integer. Sometimes, the key to answering a question correctly is identifying this constraint.

Problem Set

Solve the following problems with the four-step method outlined in this section.

1. John is 20 years older than Brian. Twelve years ago, John was twice as old as Brian. How old is Brian?

2. Caleb spends $72.50 on 50 hamburgers for the marching band. If single burgers cost $1.00 each and double burgers cost $1.50 each, how many double burgers did he buy?

3. United Telephone charges a base rate of $10.00 for service, plus an additional charge of $0.25 per minute. Atlantic Call charges a base rate of $12.00 for service, plus an additional charge of $0.20 per minute. For what number of minutes would the bills for each telephone company be the same?

4. Carina has 100 ounces of coffee divided into 5- and 10-ounce packages. If she has 2 more 5-ounce packages than 10-ounce packages, how many 10-ounce packages does she have?

5. Martin buys a pencil and a notebook for 80 cents. At the same store, Gloria buys a notebook and an eraser for $1.20, and Zachary buys a pencil and an eraser for 70 cents. How much would it cost to buy three pencils, three notebooks, and three erasers? (Assume that there is no volume discount.)

6. Andrew will be half as old as Larry in 3 years. Andrew will also be one-third as old as Jerome in 5 years. If Jerome is 15 years older than Larry, how old is Andrew?

7. A circus earned $150,000 in ticket revenue by selling 1,800 V.I.P. and Standard tickets. They sold 25% more Standard tickets than V.I.P. tickets. If the revenue from Standard tickets represents one-third of the total ticket revenue, what is the price of a V.I.P. ticket?

8. A bookshelf holds both paperback and hardcover books. The ratio of paperback books to hardcover books is 22 to 3. How many paperback books are on the shelf?

    (1) The number of books on the shelf is between 202 and 247, inclusive.
    (2) If 18 paperback books were removed from the shelf and replaced with 18 hardcover books, the resulting ratio of paperback books to hardcover books on the shelf would be 4 to 1.

9. On the planet Flarp, 3 floops equal 5 fleeps, 4 fleeps equal 7 flaaps, and 2 flaaps equal 3 fliips. How many floops are equal to 35 fliips?

Solutions

1. **32:** Let j = John's age now and let b = Brian's age now. 12 years ago, John's age was ($j - 12$) and Brian's age was ($b - 12$).

John is 20 years older than Brian $\rightarrow$ $j = b + 20$

12 years ago, John was twice as old as Brian $\rightarrow$ $(j - 12) = 2(b - 12)$

You're solving for Brian's age. Using substitution, replace j in the second equation with ($b + 20$):

$$j - 12 = 2(b - 12)$$
$$(b + 20) - 12 = 2b - 24$$
$$b + 8 = 2b - 24$$
$$32 = b$$

Alternatively, you can use a shortcut that is applicable in a specific circumstance: when they tell you the difference in age ("John is 20 years older than Brian") and they tell you that one is twice as old as the other (as this problems says occurred 12 years ago). If John is 20 years older than Brian, then John is always 20 years older than Brian, no matter how old they are. The one time, then, that John is twice as old as Brian is when Brian's age equals the age difference (20) and John's age is twice that number (40). Therefore, 12 years ago, Brian was 20. Today, he is 20 + 12 = 32 years old.

2. **45 double burgers:**

Let s = the number of single burgers purchased

Let d = the number of double burgers purchased

Caleb bought 50 burgers: Caleb spent \$72.50 in all:

$$s + d = 50 \qquad\qquad s + 1.5d = 72.50$$

Combine the two equations by subtracting equation 1 from equation 2.

$$s + 1.5d = 72.50$$
$$- (s + \quad d = 50)$$
$$\overline{\qquad 0.5d = 22.5}$$
$$d = 45$$

3. **40 minutes:**

Let x = the number of minutes.

A call made by United Telephone costs \$10.00 plus \$0.25 per minute: $10 + 0.25x$.

A call made by Atlantic Call costs \$12.00 plus \$0.20 per minute: $12 + 0.20x$.

P

Set the expressions equal to each other:

$$10 + 0.25x = 12 + 0.20x$$
$$0.05x = 2$$
$$x = 40$$

4. **6:**

Let a = the number of 5-ounce packages.
Let b = the number of 10-ounce packages.

Carina has 100 ounces of coffee:	She has two more 5-ounce packages than 10-ounce packages:
$5a + 10b = 100$	$a = b + 2$

Combine the equations by substituting the value of a from equation 2 into equation 1.

$$5(b + 2) + 10b = 100$$
$$5b + 10 + 10b = 100$$
$$15b + 10 = 100$$
$$15b = 90$$
$$b = 6$$

5. **$4.05:**

Let p = price of 1 pencil.
Let n = price of 1 notebook.
Let e = price of 1 eraser.

Martin buys a pencil and a notebook for 80 cents: $p + n\quad = 80$
Gloria buys a notebook and an eraser for $1.20, or 120 cents: $n + e = 120$
Zachary buys a pencil and an eraser for 70 cents: $p\quad + e = 70$

One approach would be to solve for the variables separately. However, notice that the Ultimate Unknown is *not* the price of any individual item but rather the *combined* price of 3 pencils, 3 notebooks, and 3 erasers. In algebraic language, you can write:

$$3p + 3n + 3e = 3(p + n + e) = ?$$

Thus, if you can find the sum of the three prices quickly, you can simply multiply by 3 and have the answer.

The three equations you are given are very similar to each other. It should occur to you to add up all the equations:

$$
\begin{array}{rcccccl}
p & + & n & & & = & 80 \\
& & n & + & e & = & 120 \\
& & & + & e & = & 70 \\
\hline
2p & + & 2n & + & 2e & = & 270
\end{array}
$$

You are now close to the Ultimate Unknown. All you need to do is multiply both sides by $\frac{3}{2}$:

$$\left(\frac{3}{2}\right)(2p + 2n + 2e) = 270\left(\frac{3}{2}\right) = \cancel{270}\,135\left(\frac{3}{\cancel{2}}\right) = 405$$

$$3p + 3n + 3e = 405$$

6. **8:** Let A = Andrew's age now, let L = Larry's age now, and let J = Jerome's age now.

Andrew will be half as old as Larry in 3 years	→	$2(A + 3) = (L + 3)$
Andrew will also be one-third as old as Jerome in 5 years	→	$3(A + 5) = J + 5$
If Jerome is 15 years older than Larry	→	$J = L + 15$

You ultimately need to find the value of A. If you replace J in the second equation with $(L + 15)$, both the first and second equations will contain the variables A and L:

$$3(A + 5) = J + 5 \qquad \rightarrow \qquad 3(A + 5) = (L + 15) + 5$$

Simplify the first two equations:

$$2(A + 3) = (L + 3) \qquad\qquad 3(A + 5) = (L + 15) + 5$$
$$2A + 6 = L + 3 \qquad\qquad\quad 3A + 15 = L + 20$$

If you subtract the first equation from the second equation, you can cancel out L, which will allow you to solve for A:

$$
\begin{array}{rl}
& 3A + 15 = L + 20 \\
- & (2A + 6 = L + 3) \\
\hline
& A + 9 = 17 \\
& A = 8
\end{array}
$$

7. **\$125:** To answer this question correctly, you need to make sure to differentiate between the price of tickets and the *quantity* of tickets sold.

Let V = # of V.I.P. tickets sold and let S = # of Standard tickets sold.

P

The question tells you that the circus sold a total of 1,800 tickets, and that the circus sold 25% more Standard tickets than V.I.P. tickets. You can create two equations:

$$V + S = 1,800 \qquad\qquad 1.25V = S$$

You can use these equations to figure out how many of each type of ticket was sold:

$$V + S = 1,800$$
$$V + (1.25V) = 1,800$$
$$2.25V = 1,800$$
$$V = 800$$

If $V = 800$, then 800 V.I.P. tickets were sold and $1,800 - 800 = 1,000$ Standard tickets were sold.

Now you need to find the cost per V.I.P. ticket. The question states that the circus earned $150,000 in ticket revenue, and that Standard tickets represented one-third of the total revenue. Therefore, Standard tickets accounted for $1/3 \times \$150,000 = \$50,000$. V.I.P. tickets then accounted for $\$150,000 - \$50,000 = \$100,000$ in revenue.

Now, you know that the circus sold 800 V.I.P. tickets for a total of $100,000. Thus, $\$100,000/800 = \$125$ per V.I.P. ticket.

8. (**D**): Say that $p = $ # of paperback books and $h = $ # of hardcover books. From the fact that $p/h = 22/3$, you can infer several things:

$p = 22x$, where x is an integer (because a fractional book is not possible).
$h = 3x$, where x is an integer.
The total number of books is $22x + 3x = 25x$, or a multiple of 25.

You could determine the value of p given any of the following: h, x, or the total number of books.

(1) SUFFICIENT: There is only one multiple of 25 between 202 and 247, so the total number of books must be 225. You could stop here, because only one possible value for the total implies only one possible value for x, and thereby only one possible value for p. The actual calculation is $x = 225/25 = 9$, so $p = 22x = (22)(9) = 198$.

(2) SUFFICIENT: From the question stem, $p/h = 22/3$. From this statement, $(p - 18)/(h + 18) = 4/1$. This gives you two equations and two unknowns, so it is possible to solve for p, and you could stop here.

However, for the sake of completeness, the calculation follows:

Cross multiply both equation: $3p = 22h$, or $h = 3p/22$, and $(p - 18) = 4(h + 18)$.

Substitute for p into the statement equation:

$$(p - 18) = 4((3p/22) + 18)$$
$$p - 18 = 6p/11 + 72$$
$$p - 6p/11 = 90$$
$$11p/11 - 6p/11 = 90$$
$$5p/11 = 90$$
$$p = (90)(11)/5$$
$$p = (18)(11) = 198$$

The correct answer is (D).

9. **8:** All of the objects in this question are completely made up, so you can't use intuition to help you convert units. Instead, you need to use the conversion factors given in the question. Start with 35 fliips, and keep converting until you end up with floops as the units:

$$35 \text{ fliips} \times \frac{2 \text{ flaaps}}{3 \text{ fliips}} \times \frac{4 \text{ fleeps}}{7 \text{ flaaps}} \times \frac{3 \text{ floops}}{5 \text{ fleeps}} = 8 \text{ floops}$$

Chapter 2
of
Word Problems

Rates & Work

In This Chapter...

Chapter 2:

Rates & Work

One common type of word problem on the GMAT is the rate problem. Rate problems come in a variety of forms on the GMAT, but all are marked by three primary components: *rate, time,* and *distance* or *work*.

These three elements are related by the following equations:

$$\textbf{Rate} \times \textbf{Time} = \textbf{Distance}$$
$$\text{OR} \qquad \textbf{Rate} \times \textbf{Time} = \textbf{Work}$$

These equations can be abbreviated as $RT = D$ or as $RT = W$. Basic rate problems involve simple manipulation of these equations.

This chapter will discuss the ways in which the GMAT makes rate situations more complicated. Often, $RT = D$ problems will involve more than one person or vehicle traveling. Similarly, many $RT = W$ problems will involve more than one worker.

Let's get started with a review of some fundamental properties of rate problems.

Basic Motion: The RTD Chart

All basic motion problems involve three elements: Rate, Time, and Distance.

Rate is expressed as a ratio of distance and time, with two corresponding units. Some examples of rates include: 30 miles per hour, 10 meters/second, 15 kilometers/day.

Time is expressed using a unit of time. Some examples of times include: 6 hours, 23 seconds, 5 months, etc.

Distance is expressed using a unit of distance. Some examples of distances include: 18 miles, 20 meters, 100 kilometers.

You can make an "RTD chart" to solve a basic motion problem. Read the problem and fill in two of the variables. Then use the $RT = D$ formula to find the missing variable. For example:

> If a car is traveling at 30 miles per hour, how long does it take to travel 75 miles?

An RTD chart is shown to the right. Fill in your RTD chart with the given information. Then solve for the time:

	Rate (miles/hr)	×	Time (hr)	=	Distance (miles)
Car	30 mi/hr	×		=	75 mi

$30t = 75$, or $t = 2.5$ hours

Matching Units in the RTD Chart

All the units in your RTD chart must match up with one another. The two units in the rate should match up with the unit of time and the unit of distance. For example:

> It takes an elevator four seconds to go up one floor. How many floors will the elevator rise in two minutes?

The rate is 1 floor/4 seconds, which simplifies to 0.25 floors/second. Note: the rate is NOT 4 seconds per floor! This is an extremely frequent error. **Always express rates as "distance over time,"** not as "time over distance."

The time is 2 minutes. The distance is unknown.

Watch out! There is a problem with this RTD chart. The rate is expressed in floors per second, but the time is expressed in minutes. This will yield an incorrect answer.

	R (floors/sec)	×	T (min)	=	D (floors)
Elevator	0.25	×	2	=	?

To correct this table, you change the time into seconds. Then all the units will match. To convert minutes to seconds, multiply 2 minutes by 60 seconds per minute, yielding 120 seconds.

	R (floors/sec)	×	T (sec)	=	D (floors)
Elevator	0.25	×	120	=	?

Once the time has been converted from 2 minutes to 120 seconds, the time unit will match the rate unit, and you can solve for the distance using the $RT = D$ equation:

$$0.25(120) = d \qquad d = 30 \text{ floors}$$

Another example:

> A train travels 90 kilometers/hr. How many hours does it take the train to travel
> 450,000 meters? (1 kilometer = 1,000 meters)

First, divide 450,000 meters by 1,000 to convert this distance to 450 km. By doing so, you match the distance unit (kilometers) with the rate unit (kilometers per hour).

	R (km/hr)	×	T (hr)	=	D (km)
Train	90	×	?	=	450

You can now solve for the time: $90t = 450$. Thus, $t = 5$ hours. Note that this time is the "stopwatch" time: if you started a stopwatch at the start of the trip, what would the stopwatch read at the end of the trip? This is not what a clock on the wall would read, but if you take the *difference* of the start and end clock times (say, 1pm and 6pm), you will get the stopwatch time of 5 hours.

The RTD chart may seem like overkill for relatively simple problems such as these. In fact, for such problems, you can simply set up the equation $RT = D$ or $RT = W$ and then substitute. However, the RTD chart comes into its own when you have more complicated scenarios that contain more than one RTD relationship, as you'll see in the next section.

Multiple Rates

Some rate questions on the GMAT will involve *more than one trip or traveler*. To deal with this, you will need to deal with multiple $RT = D$ relationships. For example:

> Harvey runs a 30-mile course at a constant rate of 4 miles per hour. If Clyde runs
> the same track at a constant rate and completes the course in 90 fewer minutes,
> how fast did Clyde run?

An RTD chart for this question would have two rows: one for Harvey and one for Clyde.

	R (miles/hr)	×	T (hr)	=	D (miles)
Harvey					
Clyde					

To answer these questions correctly, you will need to pay attention to the relationships between these two equations. By doing so, you can reduce the total number of variables you need and can solve for the desired value with the number of equations you have.

For instance, both Harvey and Clyde ran the same course, so the distance they both ran was 30 miles. Additionally, you know Clyde ran for 90 fewer minutes. To make units match, you can convert 90 minutes to 1.5 hours. If Harvey ran t hours, then Clyde ran $(t − 1.5)$ hours:

	R	×	T	=	D
	(miles/hr)		(hr)		(miles)
Harvey	4		t		30
Clyde			t − 1.5		30

Now you can solve for *t*:

$$4t = 30$$
$$t = 7.5$$

If $t = 7.5$, then Clyde ran for $7.5 - 1.5 = 6$ hours. You can now solve for Clyde's rate. Let *r* equal Clyde's rate:

$$r \times 6 = 30$$
$$r = 5$$

For questions that involve multiple rates, remember to set up multiple $RT = D$ equations and look for relationships between the equations. These relationships will help you reduce the number of variables you need and allow you to solve for the desired value.

Relative Rates

Relative rate problems are a subset of multiple rate problems. The defining aspect of relative rate problems is that two bodies are traveling *at the same time*. There are three possible scenarios:

1. The bodies move towards each other
2. The bodies move away from each other
3. The bodies move in the same direction on the same path

These questions can be dangerous because they can take a long time to solve using the conventional multiple rates strategy (discussed in the last section). You can save valuable time and energy by creating a third $RT = D$ equation for the rate at which the distance between the bodies changes:

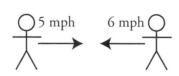 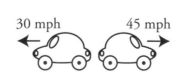 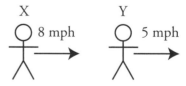

Two people decrease the distance between themselves at a rate of 5 + 6 = 11 mph. | Two cars increase the distance between themselves at a rate of 30 + 45 = 75 mph. | Persons X and Y decrease the distance between themselves at a rate of 8 − 5 = 3 mph.

Rates & Work   Chapter 2

> Imagine that two people are 14 miles apart and begin walking towards each
> other. Person A walks 3 miles per hour, and Person B walks 4 miles per hour. How
> long will it take them to reach each other?

To answer this question using multiple rates, you would need to make two important inferences: the time that each person walks is exactly the same (t hours) and the total distance they walk is 14 miles. If one person walks d miles, the other walks $(14 - d)$ miles. The chart would look like this:

	R (miles/hr)	×	T (hr)	=	D (miles)
Person A	3		t		d
Person B	4		t		$14 - d$

Alternatively, you can create an $RT = D$ equation for the rate at which they're getting closer to each other.

The rate at which they're getting closer to each other is $3 + 4 = 7$ miles per hour. In other words, after every hour they walk, they are 7 miles closer to each other. Now you can create one $RT = D$ equation:

	R (miles/hr)	×	T (hr)	=	D (miles)
A + B	7		t		14

$7t = 14$
$t = 2$

You may very well have answered this question intuitively. But as the questions become more difficult, this method only becomes more valuable. Try this problem first on your own:

> Car X is 40 miles west of Car Y. Both cars are traveling east, and Car X is going 50%
> faster than Car Y. If both cars travel at a constant rate and it takes Car X 2 hours
> and 40 minutes to catch up to Car Y, how fast is Car Y going?

A multiple rates approach to this problem is difficult. Even if you do set up the equations, they will be difficult and time-consuming to solve. The multiple RTD chart would look like this:

	R (miles/hr)	×	T (hr)	=	D (miles)
Car X	$1.5r$		$8/3$		d
Car Y	r		$8/3$		$d - 40$

Instead, you can answer this question with one equation. If Car X is initially 40 miles behind Car Y, and they both travel until Car X catches up to Car Y, then the distance between them will have de-

MANHATTAN
GMAT   35

2

creased by 40 miles. That is your distance. The distance between the two cars is decreasing at a rate of $1.5r - r = 0.5r$, and the time they travel is 8/3 hours:

$$0.5r \times \frac{8}{3} = 40$$

$$\frac{1}{2}r \times \frac{8}{3} = 40$$

$$\frac{4}{3}r = 40$$

$$r = 30$$

You defined the rate Car Y was traveling as r, so if $r = 30$, then Car Y was going 30 miles per hour.

For questions that involve relative rates, save yourself time and energy by creating an $RT = D$ equation for the rate at which the distance between the two bodies is changing.

Average Rate: Don't Just Add and Divide

Consider the following problem:

> If Lucy walks to work at a rate of 4 miles per hour, but she walks home by the same route at a rate of 6 miles per hour, what is Lucy's average walking rate for the round trip?

It is very tempting to find an average rate as you would find any other average: add and divide. Thus, you might say that Lucy's average rate is 5 miles per hour ($4 + 6 = 10$ and $10 \div 2 = 5$). However, this is incorrect!

If an object moves the **same distance** twice, but at **different rates**, then *the average rate will NEVER be the average of the two rates given for the two legs of the journey*. In fact, because the object spends more time traveling at the slower rate, *the average rate will be closer to the slower of the two rates than to the faster*.

In order to find the average rate, you must first find the *total* combined time for the trips and the *total* combined distance for the trips.

First, you need a value for the distance. Since all you need to know to determine the average rate is the *total time* and *total distance*, you can actually pick any number for the distance. The portion of the total distance represented by each part of the trip ("Going" and "Return") will dictate the time.

Pick a Smart Number for the distance. Since 12 is a multiple of the two rates in the problem, 4 and 6, 12 is an ideal choice.

Set up a multiple RTD chart:

	Rate (miles/hr)	×	Time (hr)	=	Distance (miles)
Going	4	×		=	12
Return	6	×		=	12
Total	?	×		=	24

The times can be found using the RTD equation. For the GOING trip, $4t = 12$, so $t = 3$ hrs. For the RETURN trip, $6t = 12$, so $t = 2$ hrs. Thus, the total time is 5 hrs.

	Rate (miles/hr)	×	Time (hr)	=	Distance (miles)
Going	4	×	**3**	=	12
Return	6	×	**2**	=	12
Total	?	×	**5**	=	24

Now that you have the total time and the total distance, you can find the average rate using the RTD formula:

$$RT = D$$
$$r(5) = 24$$
$$r = 4.8 \text{ miles per hour}$$

Again, 4.8 miles per hour is *not* the simple average of 4 miles per hour and 6 miles per hour. In fact, it is the weighted average of the two rates, with the *times* as the weights.

You can test different numbers for the distance (try 24 or 36) to prove that you will get the same answer, regardless of the number you choose for the distance.

Basic Work Problems

Work problems are just another type of rate problem. Instead of distances, however, these questions are concerned with the amount of "work" done.

Work: Work takes the place of distance. Instead of $RT = D$, use the equation $RT = W$. The amount of work done is often a number of jobs completed or a number of items produced.

Time: This is the time spent working.

Rate: In work problems, the rate expresses the amount of work done in a given amount of time. Rearrange the equation to isolate the rate:

$$R = \frac{W}{T}$$

Be sure to express a rate as work per time (W/T), NOT time per work (T/W). For example, if a machine produces pencils at a constant rate of 120 pencils every 30 seconds, the rate at which the machine works is $\frac{120 \text{ pencils}}{30 \text{ seconds}} = 4$ pencils/second.

Many work problems will require you to calculate a rate. Try the following problem:

> Martha can paint $\frac{3}{7}$ of a room in $4\frac{1}{2}$ hours. If Martha finishes painting the room at the same rate, how long will it have taken Martha to paint the room?
>
> (A) $8\frac{1}{3}$ hours　(B) 9 hours　(C) $9\frac{5}{7}$ hours　(D) $10\frac{1}{2}$ hours　(E) $11\frac{1}{7}$ hours

Your first step in this problem is to calculate the rate at which Martha paints the room. You can say that painting the entire room is completing 1 unit of work. Set up an *RTW* chart:

	R (rooms/hr)	×	T (hr)	=	W (rooms)
Martha	r		$\frac{9}{2}$		$\frac{3}{7}$

Now you can solve for the rate:

$$r \times \frac{9}{2} = \frac{3}{7}$$
$$r = \frac{3}{7} \times \frac{2}{9} = \frac{2}{21}$$

The division would be messy, so leave it as a fraction. Martha paints $\frac{2}{21}$ of the room every hour. Now you have what you need to answer the question. Remember, painting the whole room is the same as doing 1 unit of work. Set up another *RTW* chart:

	R (rooms/hr)	×	T (hr)	=	W (rooms)
Martha	$\frac{2}{21}$		t		1

$$\left(\frac{2}{21}\right)t = 1$$

$$t = \frac{21}{2} = 10\frac{1}{2}$$

2

The correct answer is (D). Notice that the rate and the time in this case were reciprocals of each other. This will always be true when the amount of work done is 1 unit (because reciprocals are defined as having a product of 1).

Working Together: Add the Rates

More often than not, work problems will involve more than one worker. When two or more workers are performing the same task, their rates can be added together. For instance, if Machine A can make 5 boxes in an hour, and Machine B can make 12 boxes in an hour, then working together the two machines can make 5 + 12 = 17 boxes per hour.

Likewise, if Lucas can complete 1/3 of a task in an hour and Serena can complete 1/2 of that task in an hour, then working together they can complete 1/3 + 1/2 = 5/6 of the task every hour.

If, on the other hand, one worker is undoing the work of the other, subtract the rates. For instance, if one hose is filling a pool at a rate of 3 gallons per minute, and another hose is draining the pool at a rate of 1 gallon per minute, the pool is being filled at a rate of 3 − 1 = 2 gallons per minute.

Try the following problem:

> Machine A fills soda bottles at a constant rate of 60 bottles every 12 minutes and Machine B fills soda bottles at a constant rate of 120 bottles every 8 minutes. How many bottles can both machines working together at their respective rates fill in 25 minutes?

To answer these questions quickly and accurately, it is a good idea to begin by expressing rates in equivalent units:

$$\text{Rate}_{MachineA} = \frac{60 \text{ bottles}}{12 \text{ minutes}} = 5 \text{ bottles/minute}$$

$$\text{Rate}_{MachineB} = \frac{120 \text{ bottles}}{8 \text{ minutes}} = 15 \text{ bottles/minute}$$

That means that working together they fill 5 + 15 = 20 bottles every minute. Now you can fill out an *RTW* chart. Let *b* be the number of bottles filled:

	R (bottles/min)	$\times$	T (min)	$=$	W (bottles)
$A + B$	20		25		b

$b = 20 \times 25 = 500$ bottles

Remember that, even as work problems become more complex, there are still only a few relevant relationships: $RT = W$ and $R_A + R_B = R_{A+B}$.

> Alejandro, working alone, can build a doghouse in 4 hours. Betty can build the same doghouse in 3 hours. If Betty and Carmelo, working together, can build the doghouse twice as fast as Alejandro, how long would it take Carmelo, working alone, to build the doghouse?

Begin by solving for the rate that each person works. Let c represent the number of hours it takes Carmelo to build the doghouse.

Alejandro can build $\frac{1}{4}$ of the doghouse every hour, Betty can build $\frac{1}{3}$ of the doghouse every hour, and Carmelo can build $\frac{1}{c}$ of the doghouse every hour.

The problem states that Betty and Carmelo, working together, can work twice as fast as Alejandro. That means that their rate is twice Alejandro's rate:

$$\text{Rate}_B + \text{Rate}_C = 2\left(\text{Rate}_A\right)$$
$$\frac{1}{3} + \frac{1}{c} = 2\left(\frac{1}{4}\right)$$
$$\frac{1}{c} = \frac{1}{2} - \frac{1}{3} = \frac{1}{6}$$
$$c = 6$$

It takes Carmelo 6 hours working by himself to build the doghouse.

When dealing with multiple rates, be sure to express rates in equivalent units. When the the work involves completing a task, remember to treat completing the task as doing one "unit" of work. Once you know the rates of every worker, add the rates of workers who work together on a task.

Population Problems

The final type of rate problem on the GMAT is the population problem. In such problems, some population typically increases *by a common factor* every time period. These can be solved with a **population chart**. Consider the following example:

> The population of a certain type of bacterium triples every 10 minutes. If the population of a colony 20 minutes ago was 100, in approximately how many minutes from now will the bacteria population reach 24,000?

You can solve simple population problems, such as this one, by using a population chart. Make a table with a few rows, labeling one of the middle rows as "NOW." Work forward, backward, or both (as necessary in the problem), obeying any conditions given in the problem statement about the rate of growth or decay. In this case, simply triple each population number as you move down a row. Notice that while the population increases by a constant *factor*, it does *not* increase by a constant *amount* each time period.

For this problem, the population chart at right shows that the bacterial population will reach 24,000 about 30 minutes from now.

In some cases, you might pick a Smart Number for a starting point in your population chart. If you do so, pick a number that makes the computations as simple as possible.

Time Elapsed	Population
20 minutes ago	100
10 minutes ago	300
NOW	900
in 10 minutes	2,700
in 20 minutes	8,100
in 30 minutes	24,300

Problem Set

Solve the following problems, using the strategies you have learned in this section. Use *RTD* or *RTW* charts as appropriate to organize information.

1. The population of grasshoppers doubles in a particular field every year. Approximately how many years will it take the population to grow from 2,000 grasshoppers to 1,000,000 or more?

2. Two hoses are pouring water into an empty pool. Hose 1 alone would fill up the pool in 6 hours. Hose 2 alone would fill up the pool in 4 hours. How long would it take for both hoses to fill up two-thirds of the pool?

3. An empty bucket being filled with paint at a constant rate takes 6 minutes to be filled to 7/10 of its capacity. How much more time will it take to fill the bucket to full capacity?

4   Nicky and Cristina are running a race. Since Cristina is faster than Nicky, she gives him a 36 meter head start. If Cristina runs at a pace of 5 meters per second and Nicky runs at a pace of only 3 meters per second, how many seconds will Nicky have run before Cristina catches up to him?

    (A) 15 seconds   (B) 18 seconds   (C) 25 seconds   (D) 30 seconds   (E) 45 seconds

5. Did it take a certain ship less than 3 hours to travel 9 kilometers? (1 kilometer = 1,000 meters)

    (1)   The ship's average speed over the 9 kilometers was greater than 55 meters per minute.
    (2)   The ship's average speed over the 9 kilometers was less than 60 meters per minute.

6. Twelve identical machines, running continuously at the same constant rate, take 8 days to complete a shipment. How many additional machines, each running at the same constant rate, would be needed to reduce the time required to complete a shipment by 2 days?

    (A) 2   (B) 3   (C) 4   (D) 6   (E) 9

7. Al and Barb shared the driving on a certain trip. What fraction of the total distance did Al drive?

    (1)   Al drove for 3/4 as much time as Barb did.
    (2)   Al's average driving speed for the entire trip was 4/5 of Barb's average driving speed for the trip.

8.   Mary and Nancy can each perform a certain task in *m* and *n* hours, respectively.
     Is $m < n$?

P

(1)   Twice the time it would take both Mary and Nancy to perform the task to-
      gether, each working at their respective constant rates, is greater than *m*.
(2)   Twice the time it would take both Mary and Nancy to perform the task to-
      gether, each working at their respective constant rates, is less than *n*.

Solutions

1. **9 years:** Organize the information given in a population chart. Notice that since the population is increasing exponentially, it does not take very long for the population to top 1,000,000.

Time Elapsed	Population
NOW	2,000
1 year	4,000
2 years	8,000
3 years	16,000
4 years	32,000
5 years	64,000
6 years	128,000
7 years	256,000
8 years	512,000
9 years	1,024,000

2. $1\dfrac{3}{5}$ **hours :** If Hose 1 can fill the pool in 6 hours, its rate is 1/6 "pool per hour," or the fraction of the job it can do in one hour. Likewise, if Hose 2 can fill the pool in 4 hours, its rate is 1/4 pool per hour. Therefore, the combined rate is 5/12 pool per hour (1/4 + 1/6 = 5/12):

$RT = W$
$(5/12)t = 2/3$
$t = \left(\dfrac{2}{3}\right)\left(\dfrac{12}{5}\right) = \dfrac{8}{5} = 1\dfrac{3}{5}$ hours

	R (pool/hr)	$\times$	T (hr)	$=$	W (pool)
	5/12	$\times$	t	$=$	2/3

3. $2\dfrac{4}{7}$ **minutes:** Use the $RT = W$ equation to solve for the rate, with $t = 6$ minutes and $w = \dfrac{7}{10}$:

$r(6 \text{ minutes}) = \dfrac{7}{10}$
$r = \dfrac{7}{10} \div 6 = \dfrac{7}{60}$ buckets per minute.

	R (bucket/min)	$\times$	T (min)	$=$	W (bucket)
	r	$\times$	6	$=$	7/10

Then, substitute this rate into the equation again, using 3/10 for w (the remaining work to be done):

$\left(\dfrac{7}{60}\right)t = \dfrac{3}{10}$
$t = \dfrac{3}{1\cancel{0}} \times \dfrac{6\cancel{0}}{7} = \dfrac{18}{7} = 2\,{}^4\!/_7$ minutes

	R (bucket/min)	$\times$	T (min)	$=$	W (bucket)
	7/60	$\times$	t	$=$	3/10

P

4. **(B) 18 seconds:** Save time on this problem by dealing with the rate at which the distance between Cristina and Nicky changes. Nicky is originally 36 meters ahead of Cristina. If Nicky runs at a rate of 3 meters per second and Cristina runs at a rate of 5 meters per second, then the distance between the two runners is shrinking at a rate of $5 - 3 = 2$ meters per second.

You can now figure out how long it will take for Cristina to catch Nicky using a single $RT = D$ equation. The rate at which the distance between the two runners is shrinking is 2 meters per second, and the distance is 36 meters (because that's how far apart Nicky and Cristina are):

	R ×	T =	D
	(meters/sec)	(sec)	(meters)
	2	t	36

$$2t = 36$$
$$t = 18$$

5. **(A):** Statement (1) ALONE is sufficient, but Statement (2) alone is NOT sufficient.

Notice that the statements provide rates in meters per minute. A good first step here is to figure out how fast the ship would have to travel to cover 9 kilometers in 3 hours. Create an RTD chart, and convert kilometers to meters and hours to minutes:

	R ×	T =	D
	(meters/min)	(min)	(meters)
	r	180	9,000

$$180r = 9,000$$
$$r = 50$$

The question asks whether the ship traveled 9 kilometers in *less than* 3 hours. The ship must travel faster than 50 meters/min to make it in less than 3 hours. Therefore, the question is really asking, is $r > 50$?

(1): SUFFICIENT: If the average speed of the ship was greater than 55 meters per minute, then $r > 55$. Thus, r is definitely greater than 50.

(2): INSUFFICIENT: If the average speed of the ship was less than 60 meters per minute, then $r < 60$. This is not enough information to guarantee that $r > 50$.

6. **(C):** 4 additional machines.

Let the work rate of 1 machine be r. Then the work rate of 12 machines is $12r$, and you can set up an RTW chart:

	R ×	T =	W
Original	12r	8	96r

The shipment work is then $96r$. To figure out how many machines are needed to complete this work in $8 - 2 = 6$ days, set up another row and solve for the unknown rate:

	R	×	T	=	W
Original	12r		8		96r
New			6		96r

Therefore, there are $96r/6 = 16r$ machines in total, or $16 - 12 = 4$ additional machines.

7. **(C):** Together the statements are SUFFICIENT to answer the question.

You can rephrase the question as follows: What is the ratio of Al's driving distance to the entire distance driven? Alternatively, since the entire distance is the sum of only Al's distance and Barb's distance, you can simply find the ratio of Al's distance to Barb's distance:

(1): INSUFFICIENT. You have no rate information, and so you have no definitive distance relationships:

	R	×	T	=	W
Al			(3/4)t		
Barb			t		
Total					

(2): INSUFFICIENT. As with Statement (1), you have no definitive distance relationships:

	R	×	T	=	W
Al	(4/5)r				
Barb	r				
Total					

(1) & (2) TOGETHER: SUFFICIENT:

	R	×	T	=	W
Al	(4/5)r		(3/4)t		(3/5)rt
Barb	r		t		rt
Total					(8/5)rt

Al drove $\dfrac{\frac{3}{5}rt}{\frac{8}{5}rt} = \dfrac{3}{8}$ of the distance. (Alternatively, he drove 3/5 as much as Barb did, meaning that he drove 3/8 of the trip.) Notice that you do not need the absolute time, nor the rate, of either driver's portion of the trip.

8. **(D):** EACH statement ALONE is sufficient to answer the question. First, set up an *RTW* chart:

	R	×	T	=	W
Mary	1/m		m		1
Nancy	1/n		n		1

Recall that the question is "Is $m < n$?"

(1): SUFFICIENT.

Find out how much time it would take for the task to be performed with both Mary and Nancy working:

	R	×	T	=	W
Mary	1/m		m		1
Nancy	1/n		n		1
Total	1/m + 1/n		t		1

$$\left(\frac{1}{m} + \frac{1}{n}\right)t = 1$$

$$\left(\frac{m+n}{mn}\right)t = 1$$

$$t = \frac{mn}{m+n}$$

Now, set up the inequality described in the statement (that is, twice this time is greater than *m*):

$$2t > m$$

$$2\left(\frac{mn}{m+n}\right) > m$$

$$2mn > mn + m^2 \qquad \text{You can cross multiply by } m+n \text{ because } m+n \text{ is positive.}$$

$$mn > m^2$$

$$n > m \qquad \text{You can divide by } m \text{ because } m \text{ is positive.}$$

Alternatively, you can rearrange the original inequality thus:

$$t > \frac{m}{2}$$

If both Mary and Nancy worked at Mary's rate, then together, they would complete the task in $\frac{m}{2}$ hours. Since the actual time is longer, Nancy must work more slowly than Mary, and thus $n > m$.

(2): SUFFICIENT.

You can reuse the computation of *t*, the time needed for the task to be jointly performed:

$$2t < n$$

$$2\left(\frac{mn}{m+n}\right) < n$$

$$2mn < nm + n^2 \qquad \text{Again, you can cross multiply by } m+n \text{ because } m+n \text{ is positive.}$$

$$mn < n^2$$

$$m < n \qquad \text{You can divide by } n \text{ because } n \text{ is positive.}$$

P

Alternatively, you can rearrange the original inequality thus:

$$t < \frac{n}{2}$$

If both Mary and Nancy worked at Nancy's rate, then together, they would complete the task in $\frac{n}{2}$ hours. Since the actual time is shorter, Mary must work faster than Nancy, and thus $m < n$.

Chapter 3
of
Word Problems

Statistics

In This Chapter...

Chapter 3:
Statistics

Averages

The **average** (or the **arithmetic mean**) of a set is given by the following formula:

$$\text{Average} = \frac{\text{Sum}}{\text{\# of terms}}, \text{ which is abbreviated as } A = \frac{S}{n}.$$

The sum, S, refers to the sum of all the terms in the set.
The number, n, refers to the number of terms that are in the set.
The average, A, refers to the average value (arithmetic mean) of the terms in the set.

The language in an average problem will often refer to an "arithmetic mean." However, occasionally, the concept is implied. "The cost per employee, if equally shared, is $20" means that the *average* cost per employee is $20. Likewise, the "per capita income" is the average income per person in an area.

A commonly used variation of the average formula is this:

$$(\text{Average}) \times (\text{\# of terms}) = (\text{Sum}), \text{ or } A \cdot n = S.$$

This formula has the same basic form as the $RT = D$ equation, so it lends itself readily to the same kind of table you would use for RTD problems.

Every GMAT problem dealing with averages can be solved with one of these two formulas. In general, if the average is unknown, the first formula (the definition of average) will solve the problem more directly. If the average is known, the second formula is better.

In any case, if you are asked to use or find the average of a set, you should not concentrate on the individual terms of the set. As you can see from the formulas above, all that matters is the *sum* of the terms—which can often be found even if the individual terms cannot be determined.

Using the Average Formula

The first thing to do for any GMAT average problem is to write down the average formula. Then, fill in any of the three variables (S, n, and A) that are given in the problem:

The sum of 6 numbers is 90. What is the average term?

$$A = \frac{S}{n}$$

The sum, S, is given as 90. The number of terms, n, is given as 6. By plugging in, you can solve for the average: $\frac{90}{6} = 15$

Notice that you do *not* need to know each term in the set to find the average!

Sometimes, using the average formula will be more involved. For example:

If the average of the set {2, 5, 5, 7, 8, 9, x} is 6.1, what is the value of x?

Plug the given information into the average formula, and solve for x:

$A \cdot n = S$

$$(6.1)(7 \text{ terms}) = 2 + 5 + 5 + 7 + 8 + 9 + x$$
$$42.7 = 36 + x$$
$$6.7 = x$$

More complex average problems involve setting up two average formulas. For example:

Sam earned a \$2,000 commission on a big sale, raising his average commission by \$100. If Sam's new average commission is \$900, how many sales has he made?

To keep track of two average formulas in the same problem, you can set up an RTD-style table. Instead of $RT = D$, use $A \cdot n = S$, which has the same form. Sam's new average commission is \$900, and this is \$100 higher than his old average, so his old average was \$800.

Note that the Number and Sum columns add up to give the new cumulative values, but the values in the Average column do *not* add up:

	Average	×	Number	=	Sum
Old Total	800	×	n	=	$800n$
This Sale	2000	×	1	=	2000
New Total	900	×	$n + 1$	=	$900(n + 1)$

The right-hand column gives the equation you need:

$$800n + 2000 = 900(n + 1)$$
$$800n + 2000 = 900n + 900$$
$$1100 = 100n$$
$$11 = n$$

Since you are looking for the new number of sales, which is $n + 1$, Sam has made a total of 12 sales.

MANHATTAN
GMAT

Weighted Averages

The basic formula for averages applies only to sets of data consisting of individual values, all of which are equally weighted (i.e., none of the values "counts" toward the average any more than any other value does). When you consider sets in which some data are more heavily weighted than other data—whether weighted by percents, frequencies, ratios, or fractions—you need to use special techniques for *weighted averages*.

Think about the "normal" average of 20 and 30, which equals 25. To get 25, add 20 and 30, then divide by 2. Look at the formula and manipulate it a little:

$$\frac{20+30}{2} = \frac{20}{2} + \frac{30}{2} = \frac{1}{2}(20) + \frac{1}{2}(30) = 25$$

So you can think about the average as a *sum of weighted numbers*. In this computation, the original 20 and 30 each have an equal "weight" of 1/2. To get the average (25), first multiply each number (20 and 30) by its weight (1/2 for each). Then add the results.

If you take the normal average of 20, 30, and 40, you see a similar pattern:

$$\frac{20+30+40}{3} = \frac{20}{3} + \frac{30}{3} + \frac{40}{3} = \frac{1}{3}(20) + \frac{1}{3}(30) + \frac{1}{3}(40) = 30$$

The 20, 30, and 40 each have an equal weight of 1/3. Notice that in both cases, the equal weights sum up to 1: $\frac{1}{2} + \frac{1}{2} = 1$, and $\frac{1}{3} + \frac{1}{3} + \frac{1}{3} = 1$.

What if you adjust these weights so that they are *different*, but they still sum up to 1? You will get a weighted average, which will be closer to the number with the bigger weight. For instance, in the first example, if you assign a weight of 4/5 to the 20 and a weight of 1/5 to the 30, what happens?

$$\frac{4}{5}(20) + \frac{1}{5}(30) = \frac{4 \times 20}{5} + \frac{30}{5} = 16 + 6 = 22$$

You end up with 22, which is closer to 20. You have essentially taken the average of four 20's and one 30, which will give you an answer closer to 20 than to 30.

What if the weights do not add up to 1? Then you will not get a weighted average unless you divide by the sum of the weights. For instance, if you put a weight of 2 on the 20 and a weight of 3 on the 30, you have to divide by 5 to get weights that sum to 1, as shown below. This is equivalent to taking the average of *two* 20's and *three* 30's:

$$\frac{2(20) + 3(30)}{2+3} = \frac{2}{5}(20) + \frac{3}{5}(30) = 8 + 18 = 26$$

So you can write a weighted average in either of two ways:

$$\text{Weighted average} = \frac{\text{weight}}{\text{sum of weights}}(\text{data point}) + \frac{\text{weight}}{\text{sum of weights}}(\text{data point}) + \cdots$$

$$\text{Weighted average} = \frac{(\text{weight})(\text{data point}) + (\text{weight})(\text{data point}) + \cdots}{\text{sum of weights}}$$

3

Although weighted averages differ from traditional averages, they are still averages—meaning that their values will still fall *between* the values being averaged (or between the highest and lowest of those values, if there are more than two).

A weighted average of only *two* values will fall closer to whichever value is weighted more heavily. For instance, if a drink is made by mixing 2 shots of a liquor containing 15% alcohol with 3 shots of a liquor containing 20% alcohol, then the alcohol content of the mixed drink will be closer to 20% than to 15%.

As another example, take the weighted average of 20 and 30, with weights *a* and *b*:

$$\text{Weighted average} = \frac{a}{a+b}(20) + \frac{b}{a+b}(30)$$

The weighted average will always be between 20 and 30, as long as *a* and *b* are both positive (and on the GMAT, they always have been). If *a* and *b* are integers, then you can interpret this formula as the average of *a* 20's and *b* 30's. A number line between 20 and 30 can be used to display where the weighted average will fall.

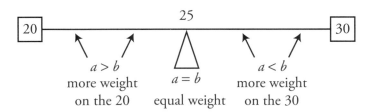

If, for example, you're told that the ratio of *a* to *b* is 3 to 1, then you know that the average will fall somewhere between 20 and 25, and you also know that it is possible to calculate the specific value. That may be enough information to answer a Data Sufficiency problem.

Finally—and importantly for Data Sufficiency problems—you do not necessarily need concrete values for the weights in a weighted-average problem. Having just the *ratios* of the weights will allow you to find a weighted average. Simply write the ratio as a fraction, and use the numerator and the denominator as weights.

Using the example of 20 and 30, you see that the ratio of the 2 weights determines the weighted average of 2 data points—and conversely, that the weighted average determines the ratio of the 2 weights. If you know one, you know the other, in theory. This principle is very useful on certain Data Sufficiency problems:

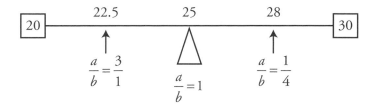

3

Alternatively, sometimes a problem will give you the data points and the average, but *not* the weights.

> A mixture of "lean" ground beef (10% fat) and "super-lean" ground beef (3% fat) has a total fat content of 8%. What is the ratio of "lean" ground beef to "super-lean" ground beef?

Fortunately, you do not need to do any complicated formulas here. You need to look at the difference between the fat contents of "lean" and "super-lean" ground beef and the fat content of the final mixture.

"Lean" ground beef has a fat content that is 2% *higher* than the fat content of the final mixture. You can say that "lean" ground beef has a +2 differential.

Similarly, "super-lean" ground beef has a fat content that is 5% *lower* than the fat content of the final mixture. You can say that "super-lean" ground beef has a −5 differential.

You need to make these differentials cancel out, so you should multiply both differentials by different numbers so that the positive will cancel out with the negative. If you were to set up an equation, it would look something like this:

$$x(+2) + y(-5) = 0$$

Now all you have to do is pick values for x and y. If $x = 5$ and $y = 2$, the equation will be true (10 + (−10) = 0). That means that for every 5 parts "lean" ground beef, you have 2 parts "super-lean" ground beef. The ratio is 5:2.

This relationship holds whenever two groups are averaged together. Suppose that A and B are averaged together. If they are in a ratio of $a:b$, then you can multiply the differential of A by a, and it will cancel out with the differential of B times b.

For instance, suppose there is a group of men and women in a ratio of 2:3. If the men have an average age of 50, and the average age of the group is 56, you can easily figure out the average age of the women in the group. Men have a −6 differential, and there are 2 of them for every 3 women. If w represents the differential between the average age of women and the average age of the group, then:

$$2 \times (-6) + 3 \times (w) = 0$$
$$-12 + 3w = 0$$
$$w = 4$$

Women have a +4 differential. The average age of the women in the group is 56 + 4 = 60 years old.

Median: The Middle Number

3

Some GMAT problems feature a second type of average: the *median*, or "middle value." The median is calculated in one of two ways, depending on the number of data points in the set:

1.   For sets containing an **odd** number of values, the median is the ***unique middle value*** when the data are arranged in increasing (or decreasing) order.

2.   For sets containing an **even** number of values, the median is the ***average (arithmetic mean) of the two middle values*** when the data are arranged in increasing (or decreasing) order.

The median of the set {5, 17, 24, 25, 28} is the unique middle number, 24. The median of the set {3, 4, 9, 9} is the mean of the two middle values (4 and 9), or 6.5. Notice that the median of a set containing an *odd* number of values must be a value in the set. However, the median of a set containing an *even* number of values does not have to be in the set—and indeed will not be, unless the two middle values are equal.

Medians of Sets Containing Unknown Values

Unlike the arithmetic mean, the median of a set depends only on the one or two values in the middle of the ordered set. Therefore, you may be able to determine a specific value for the median of a set *even if one or more unknowns are present.*

For instance, consider the unordered set {x, 2, 5, 11, 11, 12, 33}. No matter whether x is less than 11, equal to 11, or greater than 11, the median of the resulting set will be 11. (Try substituting different values of x to see why the median does not change.)

By contrast, the median of the unordered set {x, 2, 5, 11, 12, 12, 33} depends on x. If x is 11 or less, the median is 11. If x is between 11 and 12, the median is x. Finally, if x is 12 or more, the median is 12.

Entirely Unknown Sets

Occasionally, a problem may require you to construct and manipulate completely abstract sets. If this happens, you can use *alphabetical order* to make the set a little more concrete. For instance, if a question prompt states that "S is a set containing six distinct integers," then you can call those integers A, B, C,

D, *E*, and *F*, in increasing order. Alternatively, you can place the variables on an abstract number line, in order to visualize their relationships.

If the problem is complex, it may be helpful to create a **column chart**. Each column represents a number in the set. Put the columns in order, with the shortest on the left and the tallest on the right:

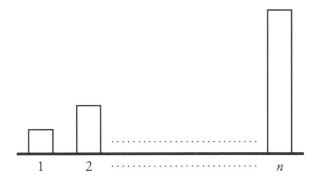

Put a column in the middle to represent the median. Add "Low/Middle/High" labels. Now you have represented an ordered set:

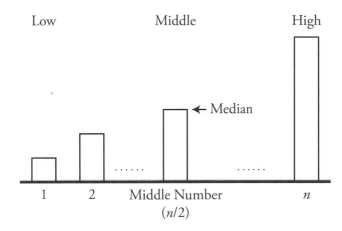

The advantage of the column chart is that it separates the values themselves from their rank, or number in the order. The values themselves are the column heights. The rank of the values is the left/right position of the columns. This way, you can see that, for instance, the top 30% of values constitute a number of columns on the right. Likewise, the bottom 10% of values are a group of columns on the far left. If you break a set up into subgroups or combine two ordered sets, you can use the same picture to guide your thinking.

Standard Deviation

The mean and median both give "average" or "representative" values for a set, but they do not tell the whole story. It is possible for two sets to have the same average but to differ widely in how spread out their values are. To describe the spread, or variation, of the data in a set, you use a different measure: the Standard Deviation.

Standard Deviation (SD) indicates how far from the average (mean) the data points typically fall. Therefore:

- A small SD indicates that a set is clustered closely around the average (mean) value.

- A large SD indicates that the set is spread out widely, with some points appearing far from the mean.

Consider the sets {5, 5, 5, 5}, {2, 4, 6, 8}, and {0, 0, 10, 10}. These sets all have the same mean value of 5. You can see at a glance, though, that the sets are very different, and the differences are reflected in their SDs. The first set has a SD of zero (no spread at all), the second set has a moderate SD, and the third set has a large SD.

	Set 1	Set 2	Set 3
	{5, 5, 5, 5}	{2, 4, 6, 8}	{0, 0, 10, 10}
Difference from the mean of 5 (in absolute terms)	{0, 0, 0, 0} average spread = 0 SD = 0 An SD of 0 means that all the numbers in the set are equal.	{3, 1, 1, 3} average spread = 2 SD = moderate (technically, SD = $\sqrt{5} \approx 2.24$)	{5, 5, 5, 5} average spread = 5 SD = large (technically, SD = 5) If every absolute difference from the mean is equal, then the SD equals that difference.

You might be asking where the $\sqrt{5}$ comes from in the technical definition of SD for the second set. The good news is that you do not need to know—**it is very unlikely that a GMAT problem will ask you to calculate an exact SD**. If you just pay attention to what the *average spread* is doing, you'll be able to answer all GMAT standard deviation problems, which involve either (a) *changes* in the SD when a set is transformed, or (b) *comparisons* of the SDs of two or more sets. Just remember that the more spread out the numbers, the larger the SD.

If you see a problem focusing on changes in the SD, ask yourself whether the changes move the data closer to the mean, farther from the mean, or neither. If you see a problem requiring comparisons, ask yourself which set is more spread out from its mean.

You should also know the term "variance," which is just the *square* of the standard deviation.

Following are some sample problems to help illustrate standard deviation properties:

1. Which set has the greater standard deviation: {1, 2, 3, 4, 5} or {440, 442, 443, 444, 445}?
2. If each data point in a set is increased by 7, does the set's standard deviation increase, decrease, or remain constant?
3. If each data point in a set is increased by a factor of 7, does the set's standard deviation increase, decrease, or remain constant? (assume that the set consists of different numbers)

3

1. The second set has the greater SD. One way to understand this is to observe that the gaps between its numbers are, on average, slightly bigger than the gaps in the first set (because the first 2 numbers are 2 units apart). Another way to resolve the issue is to observe that the set {441, 442, 443, 444, 445} would have the same standard deviation as {1, 2, 3, 4, 5}. Replacing 441 with 440, which is farther from the mean, will increase the SD.

   In any case, only the *spread* matters. The numbers in the second set are much more "consistent" in some sense—they are all within about 1% of each other, while the largest numbers in the first set are several times the smallest ones. However, this "percent variation" idea is irrelevant to the SD.

2. The SD will not change. "Increased by 7" means that the number 7 is *added* to each data point in the set. This transformation will not affect any of the gaps between the data points, and thus it will not affect how far the data points are from the mean. If the set were plotted on a number line, this transformation would merely slide the points 7 units to the right, taking all the gaps, and the mean, along with them.

3. The SD will increase. "Increased by a *factor* of 7" means that each data point is multiplied by 7. This transformation will make all the gaps between points 7 times as big as they originally were. Thus, each point will fall 7 times as far from the mean. The SD will increase by a factor of 7. Why did the problem specify that the set consists of different numbers? If each data point in the set was the same, then the SD would be 0. Multiplying each data point by 7 would still result in a set of identical numbers, and an identical SD of 0.

Problem Set

1. The average of 11 numbers is 10. When one number is eliminated, the average of the remaining numbers is 9.3. What is the eliminated number?

2. Given the set of numbers {4, 5, 5, 6, 7, 8, 21}, how much higher is the mean than the median?

3. A charitable association sold an average of 66 raffle tickets per member. Among the female members, the average was 70 raffle tickets. The male to female ratio of the association is 1:2. What was the average number of tickets sold by the male members of the association?

4. The class mean score on a test was 60, and the standard deviation was 15. If Elena's score was within 2 standard deviations of the mean, what is the lowest score she could have received?

5. Matt gets a $1,000 commission on a big sale. This commission alone raises his average commission by $150. If Matt's new average commission is $400, how many sales has Matt made?

6. If the average of x and y is 50, and the average of y and z is 80, what is the value of $z - x$?

7. On a particular exam, the boys in a history class averaged 86 points and the girls in the class averaged 80 points. If the overall class average was 82 points, what was the ratio of boys to girls in the class?

8. $S = \{1, 2, 5, 7, x\}$

    If x is a positive integer, is the mean of set S greater than 4?

    (1) The median of set S is greater than 2.
    (2) The median of set S is equal to the mean of set S.

9. {9, 12, 15, 18, 21}

    Which of the following pairs of numbers, when added to the set above, will increase the standard deviation of the set?

    I. 14, 16
    II. 9, 21
    III. 15, 100

    (A) II only   (B) III only   (C) I and II   (D) II and III   (E) I, II, and III

Solutions

1. **17:** If the average of 11 numbers is 10, their sum is $11 \times 10 = 110$. After one number is eliminated, the average is 9.3, so the sum of the 10 remaining numbers is $10 \times 9.3 = 93$. The number eliminated is the difference between these sums: $110 - 93 = 17$.

2. **2:** The mean of the set is the sum of the numbers divided by the number of terms: $56 \div 7 = 8$. The median is the middle number: 6. 8 is 2 greater than 6.

3. **58:** You can answer this question without doing a lot of calculation. Women sold an average of 70 raffle tickets, which is 4 higher than the total average of 66. Women have a +4 differential. You also know that the ratio of men to women is $1 : 2$. The women's differential multiplied by 2 will cancel with the men's differential multiplied by 1. If the men's differential is m, then:

$$1 \times m + 2 \times (+4) = 0$$
$$m + 8 = 0$$
$$m = -8$$

The men sold an average of 8 fewer tickets than the total average: $66 - 8 = 58$.

4. **30:** Elena's score was within 2 standard deviations of the mean. Since one standard deviation is 15, her score is no more than $15 \times 2 = 30$ points from the mean. The lowest possible score she could have received, then, is $60 - 30$, or 30.

5. **5:** Before the $1,000 commission, Matt's average commission was $250; you can express this algebraically with the equation $S = 250n$.

After the sale, the sum of Matt's sales increased by $1,000, the number of sales made increased by 1, and his average commission was $400. You can express this algebraically with the equation:

$$S + 1,000 = 400(n + 1)$$

$$250n + 1,000 = 400(n + 1)$$
$$250n + 1,000 = 400n + 400$$
$$150n = 600$$
$$n = 4$$

Before the big sale, Matt had made 4 sales. Including the big sale, Matt has made 5 sales.

Alternatively, you can solve this problem using the "Change to the Mean" formula.

6. **60:** The sum of two numbers is twice their average. Therefore,

$$x + y = 100 \qquad\qquad y + z = 160$$
$$x = 100 - y \qquad\qquad z = 160 - y$$

Substitute these expressions for z and x:

$$z - x = (160 - y) - (100 - y) = 160 - y - 100 + y = 160 - 100 = 60$$

Alternatively, pick Smart Numbers for x and y. Let $x = 50$ and $y = 50$ (this is an easy way to make their average equal 50). Since the average of y and z must be 80, you have $z = 110$. Therefore, $z - x = 110 - 50 = 60$.

7. **1 : 2.** The boys in the class scored 4 points higher on average than the entire class. The boys have a +4 differential. Similarly, the girls scored 2 points lower on average than the class. They have a −2 differential. You need to balance out the differentials:

$$b \times (+4) + g \times (-2) = 0$$

If $b = 1$ and $g = 2$, the equation will be true. Thus, the ratio of boys to girls is $1 : 2$.

8. **(B):** Like any other statement or question about the mean of a fixed number of data points, the prompt question can be rephrased to a question about the sum of the numbers in the set. Plug the known values into the equation Sum = Average × Number: is $(1 + 2 + 5 + 7 + x)/5 > 4$?

is $15 + x > 20$?

is $x > 5$?

For reference below, note also that the mean of S is $\dfrac{1+2+5+7+x}{5} = \dfrac{15+x}{5} = 3 + \dfrac{x}{5}$.

(1) INSUFFICIENT: For the median of the set to be greater than 2, x must also be greater than 2. If x were less than or equal to 2, the median would be 2. If x is 3 or 4, then the average of the set will be less than 4. However, if x is greater than or equal to 5, the average of the set will be greater than 4. This statement is insufficient.

(2) SUFFICIENT: This statement is a bit trickier to deal with. You can express the mean as $3 + \dfrac{x}{5}$, but the median depends on the value of x. However, note that you know the median must be an integer. You know that x must be an integer, so all of the elements in the set are integers. There are an odd number of elements in the set, so one of the elements of the set will be the median.

If the mean equals the median, then you know that $3 + \dfrac{x}{5}$ must also equal an integer. For that to be the case, you know that x must be a multiple of 5. Now you can begin testing different values of x:

x	median	mean $(3 + \dfrac{x}{5})$
5	5	4
10	5	5

$x = 10$, and the average is greater than 4. Statement 2 is sufficient.

9. **(D) II and III:** Fortunately, you do not need to perform any calculations to answer this question. The mean of the set is 15. Take a look at each Roman Numeral:

I. The numbers 14 and 16 are both very close to the mean (15). Additionally, they are closer to the mean than four of the numbers in the set, and will reduce the spread around the mean. This pair of numbers will reduce the standard deviation of the set.

II. The numbers 9 and 21 are relatively far away from the mean (15). Adding them to the list will increase the spread of the set and increase the standard deviation.

III. While adding the number 15 to the set would actually decrease the standard deviation (because it is the same as the mean of the set), the number 100 is so far away from the mean that it will greatly increase the standard deviation of the set. This pair of numbers will increase the standard deviation.

P

Chapter 4

of

Word Problems

Consecutive Integers

In This Chapter...

Chapter 4:
Consecutive Integers

Consecutive integers are integers that follow one after another from a given starting point, without skipping any integers. For example, 4, 5, 6, and 7 are consecutive integers, but 4, 6, 7, and 9 are not. There are many other types of consecutive patterns. For example:

Consecutive Even Integers: 8, 10, 12, 14 (8, 10, 14, and 16 is incorrect, as it skips 12)

Consecutive Primes: 11, 13, 17, 19 (11, 13, 15, and 17 is wrong, as 15 is not prime)

Evenly Spaced Sets

To understand consecutive integers, we should first consider sets of consecutive integers **evenly spaced sets**. These are sequences of numbers whose values go up or down by the same amount (the **increment**) from one item in the sequence to the next.

For instance, the set {4, 7, 10, 13, 16} is evenly spaced because each value increases by 3 over the previous value.

Sets of **consecutive multiples** are special cases of evenly spaced sets: all of the values in the set are multiples of the increment. For example, {12, 16, 20, 24} is a set of consecutive multiples because the values increase from one to the next by 4, and each element is a multiple of 4. Note that sets of consecutive multiples must be composed of integers.

Sets of **consecutive integers** are special cases of consecutive multiples: all of the values in the set increase by 1, and all integers are multiples

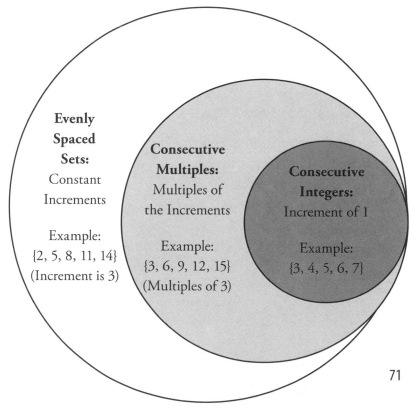

Evenly Spaced Sets: Constant Increments

Example: {2, 5, 8, 11, 14} (Increment is 3)

Consecutive Multiples: Multiples of the Increments

Example: {3, 6, 9, 12, 15} (Multiples of 3)

Consecutive Integers: Increment of 1

Example: {3, 4, 5, 6, 7}

of 1. For example, {12, 13, 14, 15, 16} is a set of consecutive integers because the values increase from one to the next by 1, and each element is an integer.

The relations among evenly spaced sets, consecutive multiples, and consecutive integers are displayed on the previous page:

4

- All sets of consecutive integers are sets of consecutive multiples.
- All sets of consecutive multiples are evenly spaced sets.
- All evenly spaced sets are fully defined if the following three parameters are known:
  1. The smallest (**first**) or largest (**last**) number in the set
  2. The **increment** (always 1 for consecutive integers)
  3. The **number of items** in the set

Properties of Evenly Spaced Sets

The following properties apply to **all** evenly spaced sets:

1. The **arithmetic mean** (average) and **median** are equal to each other. In other words, the average of the elements in the set can be found by figuring out the median, or "middle number." For example:

    What is the arithmetic mean of 4, 8, 12, 16, and 20?

    In this example you have five consecutive multiples of 4. The median is the third largest, or 12. Since this is an evenly spaced set, the arithmetic mean (average) is also 12.

    What is the arithmetic mean of 4, 8, 12, 16, 20, and 24?

    In this example you have six consecutive multiples of 4. The median is the arithmetic mean (average) of the third largest and fourth largest, or the average of 12 and 16. Thus, the median is 14. Since this is an evenly spaced set, the average is also 14.

2. The **mean** and **median** of the set are equal to the **average** of the FIRST and LAST terms. For example:

    What is the arithmetic mean of 4, 8, 12, 16, and 20?

    In this example, 20 is the largest (last) number and 4 is the smallest (first). The arithmetic mean and median are therefore equal to $(20 + 4) \div 2 = 12$.

    What is the arithmetic mean of 4, 8, 12, 16, 20, and 24?

In this example, 24 is the largest (last) number and 4 is the smallest (first). The arithmetic mean and median are therefore equal to $(24 + 4) \div 2 = 14$.

Thus for all evenly spaced sets, just remember: the average equals (**First + Last**) $\div$ **2**.

3. The **sum** of the elements in the set equals the **arithmetic mean** (average) number in the set times the **number of items** in the set.

This property applies to all sets, but it takes on special significance in the case of evenly spaced sets because the "average" is not only the arithmetic mean, but also the median. For example:

What is the sum of 4, 8, 12, 16, and 20?

You have already calculated the average above; it is equal to 12. There are five terms, so the sum equals $12 \times 5 = 60$.

What is the sum of 4, 8, 12, 16, 20, and 24?

You have already calculated the average above; it is equal to 14. There are six terms, so the sum equals $14 \times 6 = 84$.

Counting Integers: Add One Before You Are Done

How many integers are there from 6 to 10? Four, right? Wrong! There are actually five integers from 6 to 10. Count them and you will see: 6, 7, 8, 9, 10. It is easy to forget that you have to include (or, in GMAT lingo, **be inclusive of**) extremes. In this case, both extremes (the numbers 6 and 10) must be counted. When you merely subtract $(10 - 6 = 4)$, you are forgetting to include the first extreme (6), as it has been subtracted away (along with 5, 4, 3, 2, and 1).

Do you have to methodically count each term in a long consecutive pattern? No. Just remember that if both extremes should be counted, you need to **add one before you are done**. For example:

How many integers are there from 14 to 765, inclusive?

Just remember: for consecutive integers, the formula is (**Last − First + 1**). $765 - 14$, plus 1, yields 752.

This works easily enough if you are dealing with consecutive integers. Sometimes, however, the question will ask about consecutive multiples. For example, "How many multiples of 4…" or "How many even numbers…" are examples of sets of consecutive multiples.

In this case, if you just subtract the largest number from the smallest and add one, you will be overcounting. For example, "All of the even integers between 12 and 24" yields 12, 14, 16, 18, 20, 22, and

24. That is 7 even integers. However, (Last − First + 1) would yield (24 − 12 + 1) = 13, which is too large. How do you amend this? Since the items in the list are going up by increments of 2 (you are counting only the even numbers), you need to divide (Last − First) by 2. Then, add the one before you are done:

$$(\text{Last} - \text{First}) \div \text{Increment} + 1 = (24 - 12) \div 2 + 1 = 6 + 1 = 7$$

Just remember: for consecutive multiples, the formula is **(Last − First) ÷ Increment + 1**. The bigger the increment, the smaller the result, because there is a larger gap between the numbers you are counting.

Sometimes, however, it is easier to list the terms of a consecutive pattern and count them, especially if the list is short or if one or both of the extremes are omitted. For example:

How many multiples of 7 are there between 100 and 150?

Here it may be easiest to list the multiples: 105, 112, 119, 126, 133, 140, 147. Count the number of terms to get the answer: 7. Alternatively, you could note that 105 is the first number, 147 is the last number, and 7 is the increment:

$$\text{Number of terms} = (\text{Last} - \text{First}) \div \text{Increment} + 1 = (147 - 105) \div 7 + 1 = 6 + 1 = 7$$

The Sum of Consecutive Integers

Consider this problem:

What is the sum of all the integers from 20 to 100, inclusive?

Adding all those integers would take much more time than you have for a GMAT problem. Using the rules for evenly spaced sets mentioned before, you can use shortcuts:

- Average the first and last term to find the precise "middle" of the set: 100 + 20 = 120 and 120 ÷ 2 = 60.
- Count the number of terms: 100 − 20 = 80, plus 1 yields 81.
- Multiply the "middle" number by the number of terms to find the sum: 60 × 81 = 4,860.

There are a couple of general facts to note about sums and averages of evenly spaced sets (especially sets of consecutive integers):

- The average of an **odd** number of consecutive integers (1, 2, 3, 4, 5) will always be an integer (3). This is because the "middle number" will be a single integer.
- On the other hand, the average of an **even** number of consecutive integers (1, 2, 3, 4) will never be an integer (2.5), because there is no true "middle number."

- This is because consecutive integers alternate between EVEN and ODD numbers. Therefore, the "middle number" for an even number of consecutive integers is the AVERAGE of two consecutive integers, which is never an integer.

Consider this Data Sufficiency problem:

Is k^2 odd?

    (1) $k - 1$ is divisible by 2.
    (2) The sum of k consecutive integers is divisible by k.

Statement (1) tells you that $k - 1$ is even. Therefore, k is odd, so k^2 will be odd. SUFFICIENT.

Statement (2) tells you that the sum of k consecutive integers is divisible by k. Therefore, this sum divided by k is an integer. Moreover, the sum of k consecutive integers divided by k is the average (arithmetic mean) of that set of k integers. As a result, Statement (2) is telling you that the average of the k consecutive integers is itself an integer:

$$\frac{(\text{Sum of } k \text{ integers})}{k} = (\text{Average of } k \text{ integers}) = \textbf{Integer}$$

If the average of this set of consecutive integers is an integer, then k must be odd. SUFFICIENT.

The correct answer is **(D)**. EACH statement ALONE is sufficient.

Problem Set

Solve these problems using the rules for consecutive integers.

1.   If x, y, and z are consecutive integers, is $x + y + z$ divisible by 3?

2.   What is the sum of all the positive integers up to 100, inclusive?

3.   In a sequence of 8 consecutive integers, how much greater is the sum of the last four integers than the sum of the first four integers?

4.   If the sum of a set of 10 consecutive integers is 195, what is the average of the set?

5.   How many terms are there in the set of consecutive integers from −18 to 33, inclusive?

6.   If the sum of the last 3 integers in a set of 6 consecutive integers is 624, what is the sum of the first 3 integers of the set?

7.   If the sum of the last 3 integers in a set of 7 consecutive integers is 258, what is the sum of the first 4 integers?

8.   The operation $\Longrightarrow$ is defined by $x \Longrightarrow y = x + (x + 1) + (x + 2) \ldots + y$. For example, $3 \Longrightarrow 7 = 3 + 4 + 5 + 6 + 7$. What is the value of $(100 \Longrightarrow 150) - (125 \Longrightarrow 150)$?

P

Solutions

1. **YES:** For any odd number of consecutive integers, the sum of those integers is divisible by the number of integers. There are three consecutive integers (x, y, and z), so the rule applies in this case.

2. **5,050:** There are 100 integers from 1 to 100, inclusive: $(100 - 1) + 1$. (Remember to add one before you are done.) The number exactly in the middle is 50.5. (You can find the middle term by averaging the first and last terms of the set.) Therefore, multiply 100 by 50.5 to find the sum of all the integers in the set: $100 \times 50.5 = 5,050$.

3. **16:** Think of the set of eight consecutive integers as follows: n, $(n + 1)$, $(n + 2)$, $(n + 3)$, $(n + 4)$, $(n + 5)$, $(n + 6)$, and $(n + 7)$.

First, find the sum of the first four integers:

$$n + (n + 1) + (n + 2) + (n + 3) = 4n + 6$$

Then, find the sum of the next four integers:

$$(n + 4) + (n + 5) + (n + 6) + (n + 7) = 4n + 22$$

The difference between these two partial sums is:

$$(4n + 22) - (4n + 6) = 22 - 6 = 16$$

Another way you could solve this algebraically is to line up the algebraic expressions for each number so that you can subtract one from the other directly:

Sum of the last four integers:
Less the sum of the first four integers:

$$(n + 4) + (n + 5) + (n + 6) + (n + 7)$$
$$- \ [n \quad + (n + 1) + (n + 2) + (n + 3)]$$
$$4 + \quad 4 + \quad 4 + \quad 4 \ = 16$$

Yet another way to see this outcome is to represent the eight consecutive unknowns with eight lines:

— — — —⋮— — — —

Each of the first four lines can be matched with one of the second four lines, each of which is 4 greater:

— — — —⋮+4 +4 +4 +4

So the sum of the last four numbers is $4 \times 4 = 16$ greater than the sum of the first four.

Finally, you could pick numbers to solve this problem. For example, assume you pick 1, 2, 3, 4, 5, 6, 7, and 8. The sum of the first four numbers is 10. The sum of the last four integers is 26. Again, the difference is $26 - 10 = 16$.

4. **19.5:** Average = $\dfrac{\text{Sum}}{\text{\# of terms}}$. In this problem, you have $\dfrac{195}{10} = 19.5$ as the average.

5. **52:** $33 - (-18) = 51$. Then add one before you are done: $51 + 1 = 52$.

6. **615:** Think of the set of integers as n, $(n + 1)$, $(n + 2)$, $(n + 3)$, $(n + 4)$, and $(n + 5)$. Thus, $(n + 3) + (n + 4) + (n + 5) = 3n + 12 = 624$. Therefore, $n = 204$.

The sum of the first three integers is: $204 + 205 + 206 = 615$.

Alternatively, another way you could solve this algebraically is to line up the algebraic expressions for each number so that you can subtract one from the other directly:

Sum of the last three integers: $(n + 3) + (n + 4) + (n + 5)$

Less the sum of the first three integers: $-\ [n \qquad + (n + 1) + (n + 2)]$

$$3 + \qquad 3 + \qquad 3 = 9$$

Thus, the sum of the last three numbers is 9 greater than the sum of the first three numbers, so the sum of the first three numbers is $624 - 9 = 615$.

Visusally, you can represent the six consecutive unknowns with six lines:

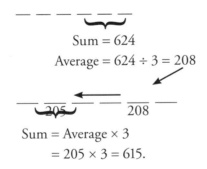

Sum = 624

Average = $624 \div 3 = 208$

Sum = Average × 3

$= 205 \times 3 = 615$.

7. **330:** Think of the set of integers as n, $(n + 1)$, $(n + 2)$, $(n + 3)$, $(n + 4)$, $(n + 5)$, and $(n + 6)$. $(n + 4) + (n + 5) + (n + 6) = 3n + 15 = 258$. Therefore, $n = 81$. The sum of the first four integers is $81 + 82 + 83 + 84 = 330$.

Alternatively: the sum of the first four integers is $4n + 6$. If $n = 81$, then $4n + 6 = 4(81) + 6 = 330$.

8. **2,800:** This problem contains two components: the sum of all the numbers from 100 to 150, and the sum of all the numbers from 125 to 150. Since you are finding the difference between these components, you are essentially finding just the sum of all the numbers from 100 to 124. You can think of this logically by solving a simpler problem: find the difference (1 ==> 5) − (3 ==> 5).

MANHATTAN
GMAT

$$\begin{array}{r}
1+2+3+4+5 \\
- \qquad\quad 3+4+5 \\
\hline
1+2
\end{array}$$

There are 25 numbers from 100 to 124 (124 − 100 + 1). Remember to add one before you are done! To find the sum of these numbers, multiply by the average term: (100 + 124) ÷ 2.

$$\frac{100+124}{2}=112$$

$$25\times112=2,800$$

P

Chapter 5
of Word Problems

Overlapping Sets

In This Chapter...

Chapter 5:
Overlapping Sets

Translation problems which involve two or more given sets of data that partially intersect with each other are termed Overlapping Sets. For example:

> 30 people are in a room. 20 of them play golf. 15 of them play golf and tennis. If everyone plays at least one of the two sports, how many of the people play tennis only?

This problem involves two sets: (1) people who play golf, and (2) people who play tennis. The two sets overlap because some of the people who play golf also play tennis. Thus, these two sets can actually be divided into four categories:

(1)   People who only play golf   (3)   People who play golf and tennis
(2)   People who only play tennis   (4)   People who play neither sport

Solving double-set GMAT problems, such as in the example above, involves finding values for these four categories.

The Double-Set Matrix

For GMAT problems involving only *two* categorizations or decisions, the most efficient tool is the *Double-Set Matrix,* a table whose rows correspond to the options for one decision, and whose columns correspond to the options for the other decision. The last row and the last column contain totals, so the bottom right corner contains the total number of everything or everyone in the problem.

Even if you are accustomed to using Venn diagrams for these problems, you should switch to the double-set matrix for problems with only two sets of options. The double-set matrix conveniently displays *all* possible combinations of options, including totals, whereas the Venn diagram only displays a few of them easily.

Of 30 integers, 15 are in set A, 22 are in set B, and 8 are in both set A and B. How many of the integers are in NEITHER set A nor set B?

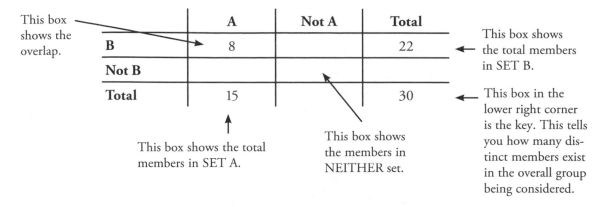

This box shows the overlap.

This box shows the total members in SET B.

This box in the lower right corner is the key. This tells you how many distinct members exist in the overall group being considered.

This box shows the total members in SET A.

This box shows the members in NEITHER set.

Once the information given in the problem has been filled in, complete the chart, using the totals to guide you. (Each row and each column sum to a total value.)

	A	Not A	Total
B	8	14	22
Not B	7	1	8
Total	15	15	30

The question asks for the number of integers that are *neither* set. Look at the chart to find the number of integers that are NOT A and NOT B; you'll find that the answer is 1.

When you construct a double-set matrix, be careful! As mentioned above, the rows should correspond to the *mutually exclusive options* for one decision. Likewise, the columns should correspond to the mutually exclusive options for the other. For instance, if a problem deals with students getting either right or wrong answers on problems 1 and 2, the columns should **not** be "problem 1" and "problem 2," and the rows should **not** be "right" and "wrong." Instead, the columns should list options for *one* decision—problem 1 correct, problem 1 incorrect, total—and the rows should list options for the other decision—problem 2 correct, problem 2 incorrect, total.

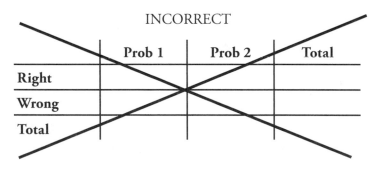

INCORRECT

	Prob 1	Prob 2	Total
Right			
Wrong			
Total			

MANHATTAN
GMAT

CORRECT

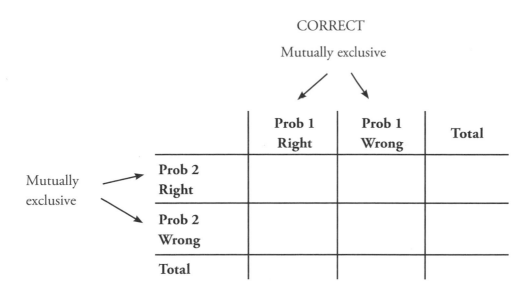

Mutually exclusive

	Prob 1 Right	Prob 1 Wrong	Total
Prob 2 Right			
Prob 2 Wrong			
Total			

5

Overlapping Sets and Percents

Many overlapping-sets problems involve *percents* or *fractions*. The double-set matrix is still effective on these problems, especially if you pick a Smart Number for the grand total. For problems involving percents, pick a total of 100. For problems involving fractions, pick a common denominator for the total. For example, pick 15 or 30 if the problem mentions categories that are 1/3 and 2/5 of the total.

> 70% of the guests at Company X's annual holiday party are employees of Company X. 10% of the guests are women who are not employees of Company X. If half the guests at the party are men, what percent of the guests are female employees of Company X?

First, fill in 100 for the total number of guests at the party. Then, fill in the other information given in the problem: 70% of the guests are employees, and 10% are women who are not employees. You also know that half the guests are men. (Therefore, you also know that half the guests are women.)

	Men	Women	Total
Employee			70
Not Emp.		10	
Total	50	50	100

Next, calculate the rest of the information in the matrix:

      100 − 70 = 30 guests who are not employees

      30 − 10 = 20 men who are not employees

      50 − 10 = 40 female employees

      50 − 20 = 30 male employees

	Men	Women	TOTAL
Employee	30	40	70
Not Emp.	20	10	30
TOTAL	50	50	100

Thus, 40% of the guests at the party are female employees of Company X. Note that the problem does not require you to complete the matrix with the number of male employees, since you have already answered the question asked in the problem. However, completing the matrix is an excellent way to check your computation. The last box you fill in must work both vertically and horizontally.

As in other problems involving Smart Numbers, you can only assign a number to the total if it is *undetermined* to start with. If the problem contains only fractions and/or percents, but no actual *numbers* of items or people, then go ahead and pick a total of 100 (for percent problems) or a common denominator (for fraction problems). But if actual quantities appear anywhere in the problem, then all the totals are already determined. In that case, you cannot assign numbers, but must solve for them instead.

Overlapping Sets and Algebraic Representation

When solving overlapping sets problems, you must pay close attention to the wording of the problem. For example, consider the problem below:

> Santa estimates that 10% of the children in the world have been good this year but do not celebrate Christmas, and that 50% of the children who celebrate Christmas have been good this year. If 40% of the children in the world have been good, what percentage of children in the world are not good and do not celebrate Christmas?

It is tempting to fill in the number 50 to represent the percent of good children who celebrate Christmas. However, this approach is incorrect.

Notice that you are told that 50% of the children *who celebrate Christmas* have been good. This is different from being told that 50% of the children in the world have been good. In this problem, the information you have is a fraction of an unknown number. You do not yet know how many children celebrate Christmas. Therefore, you cannot yet write a number for the good children who celebrate Christmas. Instead, you represent the unknown total number

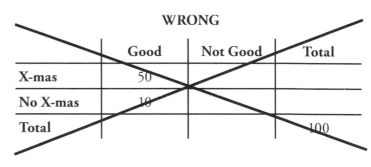

WRONG

	Good	Not Good	Total
X-mas	50		
No X-mas	10		
Total			100

CORRECT

	Good	Not Good	Total
X-mas	0.5x		x
No X-mas	10		
Total	40		100

of children who celebrate Christmas with the variable *x*. Thus, you can represent the number of good children who celebrate Christmas with the expression 0.5*x*.

From the relationships in the table, you can set up an equation to solve for *x*:

$$0.5x + 10 = 40$$
$$x = 60$$

With this information, you can fill in the rest of the table:

	Good	Not Good	Total
X-mas	$0.5x = 30$	30	$x = 60$
No X-mas	10	30	40
Total	40	60	100

Therefore, 30% of the children are not good and do not celebrate Christmas.

2 Sets, 3 Choices: Still Double-Set Matrix

Very rarely, you might need to consider more than two options for one or both of the dimensions of your chart. As long as each set of distinct options is complete and has no overlaps, you can simply extend the chart.

For instance, if respondents can answer "Yes," "No," or "Maybe" to a survey question, and you care about the gender of the respondents, then you might set up the following matrix:

	Yes	No	Maybe	Total
Female				
Male				
Total				

The set of three answer choices is complete (there are no other options). Also, the choices do not overlap (no respondent can give more than one response). So, this extended chart is fine.

You rarely need to do real computation, but setting up an extended chart such as this can be helpful on certain Data Sufficiency problems, so that you can see what information is or is not sufficient to answer the given question.

3-Set Problems: Venn Diagrams

Problems that involve three overlapping sets can be solved by using a Venn Diagram. The three overlapping sets are usually three teams or clubs, and each person is either *on* or *not on* any given team or club. That is, there are only two choices for any club: member or not. For example:

> Workers are grouped by their areas of expertise and are placed on at least one team. There are 20 workers on the Marketing team, 30 on the Sales team, and 40 on the Vision team. 5 workers are on both the Marketing and Sales teams, 6 workers are on both the Sales and Vision teams, 9 workers are on both the Marketing and Vision teams, and 4 workers are on all three teams. How many workers are there in total?

In order to solve this problem, use a Venn Diagram. A Venn Diagram should be used ONLY for problems that involve three sets. Stick to the double-set matrix for two-set problems.

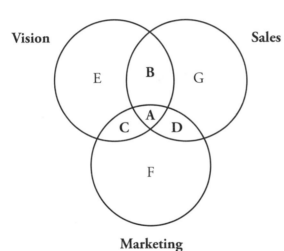

Begin your Venn Diagram by drawing three overlapping circles and labeling each one.

Notice that there are seven different sections in a Venn Diagram. There is one innermost section (**A**) where all three circles overlap. This contains individuals who are on all three teams.

There are three sections (**B, C, and D**) where two circles overlap. These contain individuals who are on two teams. There are three non-overlapping sections (**E, F, and G**) that contain individuals who are on only one team.

Venn Diagrams are easy to work with, if you remember one simple rule: **Work from the inside out.**

That is, it is easiest to begin by filling in a number in the innermost section (**A**). Then, fill in numbers in the middle sections (**B, C, and D**). Fill in the outermost sections (**E, F, and G**) last.

First: <u>Workers on all three teams.</u> Fill in the innermost circle. This is given in the problem as 4.

Second: <u>Workers on two teams.</u> Here you must remember to subtract those workers who are on all three teams. For example, the problem says that there are 5 workers on the Marketing and Sales teams.

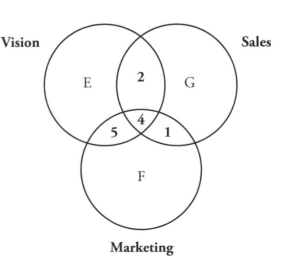

However, this includes the 4 workers who are on all three teams. Therefore, in order to determine the number of workers who are on the Marketing and Sales teams exclusively, you must subtract the 4 workers who are on all three teams. You are left with $5 - 4 = 1$. The number of workers on the Marketing and Vision teams exclusively is $9 - 4 = 5$. The number of workers on the Sales and Vision teams exclusively is $6 - 4 = 2$.

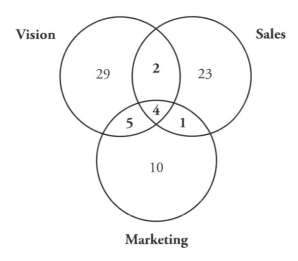

Third: <u>Workers on one team only.</u> Here you must remember to subtract those workers who are on two teams and those workers who are on three teams. For example, the problem says that there are 20 workers on the Marketing team. But this includes the 1 worker who is on the Marketing and Sales teams, the 5 workers who are on the Marketing and Vision teams, and the 4 workers who are on all three teams. You must subtract all of these workers to find that there are $20 - 1 - 5 - 4 = 10$ people who are on the Marketing team exclusively. There are $30 - 1 - 2 - 4 = 23$ people on the Sales team exclusively. There are $40 - 2 - 5 - 4 = 29$ people on the Vision team exclusively.

In order to determine the total, just add all seven numbers together = 74 total workers.

Problem Set

1.   X and Y are sets of integers. X | Y denotes the set of integers that belong to set X or set Y, but not both. If X consists of 10 integers, Y consists of 18 integers, and 5 of the integers are in both X and Y, then X | Y consists of how many integers?

2.   Of 28 people in a park, 12 are children and the rest are adults. 8 people have to leave at 3pm; the rest do not. If after 3pm, there are 6 children still in the park, how many adults are still in the park?

3.   Of 30 snakes at the reptile house, 10 have stripes, 21 are poisonous, and 5 have no stripes and are not poisonous. How many of the snakes have stripes AND are poisonous?

4.   Students are in clubs as follows: Science–20, Drama–30, and Band–12. No student is in all three clubs, but 8 are in both Science and Drama, 6 are in both Science and Band, and 4 are in Drama and Band. How many different students are in at least one of the three clubs?

5.   40% of all high school students hate roller coasters; the rest love them. 20% of those students who love roller coasters own chinchillas. What percentage of students love roller coasters but do not own a chinchilla?

6.   Of 60 children, 30 are happy, 10 are sad, and 20 are neither happy nor sad. There are 20 boys and 40 girls. If there are 6 happy boys and 4 sad girls, how many boys are neither happy nor sad?

7.   10% of all aliens are capable of intelligent thought and have more than 3 arms, and 75% of aliens with 3 arms or less are capable of intelligent thought. If 40% of all aliens are capable of intelligent thought, what percent of aliens have more than 3 arms?

8.   The 38 movies in the video store fall into the following three categories: 10 action, 20 drama, and 18 comedy. However, some movies are classified under more than one category: 5 are both action and drama, 3 are both action and comedy, and 4 are both drama and comedy. How many action–drama–comedy movies are there?

P

Solutions

1. 18: Use a Double-Set Matrix to solve this problem. First, fill in the numbers given in the problem: There are 10 integers in set X and 18 integers in set Y. There are 5 integers that are in both sets. Then, use subtraction to figure out that there are 5 integers that are in set X and not in set Y, and 13 integers that are in set Y and not in set X. This is all the information you need to solve this problem: X | Y = 5 + 13 = 18.

	Set X	NOT Set X	Total
Set Y	5	**13**	18
NOT Set Y	**5**		
Total	10		

2. 14: Use a Double-Set Matrix to solve this problem. First, fill in the numbers given in the problem: 28 total people in the park, 12 children and the rest (16) adults; 8 leave at 3pm and the rest (20) stay. Then, we are told that there are 6 children left in the park after 3pm. Since we know there are a total of 20 people in the park after 3pm, the remaining 14 people must be adults.

	Children	Adults	Total
Leave at 3			8
Stay	6	**14**	**20**
Total	12	**16**	28

3. 6: Use a Double-Set Matrix to solve this problem. First, fill in the numbers given in the problem: 30 snakes, 10 with stripes (and therefore 20 without), 21 that are poisonous (and therefore 9 that are not), and 5 that are neither striped nor poisonous. Use subtraction to fill in the rest of the chart. Thus, 6 snakes have stripes and are poisonous.

	Stripes	No Stripes	Total
Poisonous	6		21
NOT Poison	4	5	**9**
Total	10	**20**	30

4. 44: There are three overlapping sets here. Therefore, use a Venn Diagram to solve the problem. First, fill in the numbers given in the problem, working from the inside out: no students in all three clubs, 8 in Science and Drama, 6 in Science and Band, and 4 in Drama and Band. Then, use the totals for each club to determine how many students are in only one club. For example, you know that there are 30 students in the Drama club. So far, you have placed 12 students in the circle that represents the Drama club (8 who are in Science and Drama, and 4 who are in Band and Drama). Therefore, 30 − 12 = 18, the number of students who are in only the Drama Club. Use this process to determine the number of students in just the Science and Band clubs as well. To find the number of students in at least one of the clubs, sum all the numbers in the diagram:

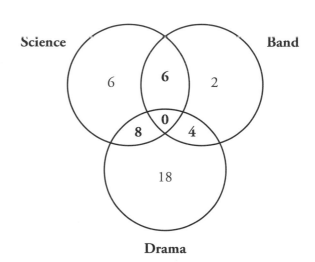

6 + 18 + 2 + 6 + 8 + 4 = 44.

5. 48: Since all the numbers in this problem are given in percentages, assign a grand total of 100 students. You know that 40% of all high school students hate roller coasters, so fill in 40 for this total and 60 for the number of students who love roller coasters. You also know that 20% **of those students who love**

	Love RCs	Do not	Total
Chinchilla	12		
No Chinch.	48		
Total	60	40	100

roller coasters own chinchillas. It does not say that 20% of all students own chinchillas. Since 60% of students love roller coasters, 20% of 60% own chinchillas. Therefore, fill in 12 for the students who both love roller coasters and own chinchillas. The other 48 roller coaster lovers do not own chinchillas.

6. 8: Use a Double-Set Matrix to solve this problem, with the "mood" set divided into three categories instead of only two. First, fill in the numbers given in the problem: of 60 children, 30 are happy, 10 are sad, and 20 are neither happy nor sad; 20 are boys and 40 are girls. You also know there are 6 happy boys and 4 sad girls. Therefore, by subtraction, there are 6 sad boys and there are 8 boys who are neither happy nor sad.

	Happy	Sad	Neither	Total
Boys	6	6	8	20
Girls		4		40
Total	30	10	20	60

7. 60%: Since all the numbers in this problem are given in percentages, assign a grand total of 100 aliens. You know that 10% of all aliens are capable of intelligent thought and have more than 3 arms. You also know that 75% **of aliens with 3 arms or less** are capable of intelligent thought. It does not say that 75% of all aliens

	Thought	No Thought	Total
> 3 arms	10		$100 - x$
≤ 3 arms	$0.75x$		x
Total	40		100

are capable of intelligent thought. Therefore, assign the variable x to represent the percentage of aliens with three arms or less. Then, the percentage of aliens with three arms or less who are capable of intelligent thought can be represented by $0.75x$. Since you know that 40% of all aliens are capable of intelligent thought, you can write the equation $10 + 0.75x = 40$, or $0.75x = 30$. Solve for x: $x = 40$. Therefore, 40% of the aliens have three arms or less, and 60% of aliens have more than three arms.

8. 2: There are three overlapping sets here; therefore, use a Venn Diagram to solve the problem. First, fill in the numbers given in the problem, working from the inside out. Assign the variable x to represent the number of action–drama–comedy movies. Then, create variable expressions, using the totals given in the problem, to represent the number of movies in each of the other categories.

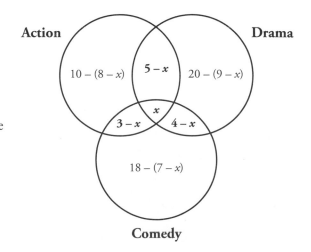

You know that there is a total of 38 movies; therefore, you can write the following equation to represent the total number of movies in the store:

$$10 - 8 + x$$
$$20 - 9 + x$$
$$18 - 7 + x$$
$$5 - x$$
$$4 - x$$
$$3 - x$$

$$+ \quad\quad x$$
$$\overline{}$$
$$36 + x = 38$$
$$x = 2$$

If you are unsure of the algebraic solution, you can also guess a number for x and fill in the rest of the diagram until the total number of movies reaches 38.

P

Chapter 6
of
Word Problems

Word Problem Strategies

In This Chapter...

Chapter 6:
Word Problem Strategies

The following five sections appear in all 5 quant strategy guides. If you are familiar with this information, skip ahead to page 108 for new content.

Data Sufficiency Basics

Every Data Sufficiency problem has the *same* basic form:

The **Question Stem** is (sometimes) made up of two parts:

(1) The **Question**: *"What day of the week is the party on?"*
(2) Possible **Additional Info**: *"Jon's birthday party is this week."*
   This might simply be background OR could provide additional constraints or equations needed to solve the problem.

Jon's birthday party is this week. What day of the week is the party on?

(1)   The party is not on Monday or Tuesday.
(2)   The party is not on Wednesday, Thursday, or Friday.

(A)   Statement (1) ALONE is sufficient, but statement (2) is NOT sufficient
(B)   Statement (2) ALONE is sufficient, but statement (1) is NOT sufficient
(C)   BOTH statements TOGETHER are sufficient, but NEITHER statement ALONE is sufficient
(D)   EACH statement ALONE is sufficient
(E)   Statements (1) and (2) TOGETHER are NOT sufficient

Following the question are **two Statements** labeled (1) and (2).

To answer Data Sufficiency problems correctly, you need to decide **whether the statements provide enough information to answer the question**. In other words, do you have *sufficient data*?

Lastly, we are given the **Answer Choices**.

These are the *same* for every Data Sufficiency problem so **memorize them** as soon as possible.

What Does "Sufficient" Mean?

The key to Data Sufficiency is to remember that it *does not* require you to answer the question asked in the question stem. Instead, you need to decide whether the statements provide enough information to answer the question.

Notice that in answer choices (A), (B), and (D), you are asked to evaluate each of the statements separately. You must then decide if the information given in each is sufficient (on its own) to answer the question in the stem.

The correct answer choice will be:

(A) when Statement (1) provides enough information by itself, but Statement (2) does not,

(B) when Statement (2) provides enough information by itself, but Statement (1) does not,

OR

(D) when BOTH statements, *independently*, provide enough information.

But what happens when you cannot answer the question with *either* statement individually? Now you must put them together and decide if all of the information given is sufficient to answer the question in the stem.

If you **must** use the statements together, the correct answer choice will be:

(C) if together they provide enough information (but neither alone is sufficient),

OR

(E) if the statements, even together, do not provide enough information.

We will revisit the answer choices when we discuss a basic process for Data Sufficiency.

The DS Process

Data Sufficiency tests logical reasoning as much as it tests mathematical concepts. In order to master Data Sufficiency, develop a consistent process that will help you stay on task. It is very easy to forget what you are actually trying to accomplish as you answer these questions.

To give yourself the best chance of consistently answering DS questions correctly, you need to be methodical. The following steps can help reduce errors on every DS problem.

Step 1: Separate *additional info* from the *actual question*.

If the additional information contains *constraints* or *equations*, make a note on your scrap paper.

Step 2: Determine whether the question is Value or Yes/No.

Value: The **question** asks for the value of an unknown (e.g., What is *x*?).

> A statement is **Sufficient** when it provides **1 possible value**.
> A statement is **Not Sufficient** when it provides **more than 1 possible value**.

Yes/No: The **question** that is asked has two possible answers: Yes or No (e.g., Is *x* even?).

> A statement is **Sufficient** when it provides a **definite Yes or definite No**.
> A statement is **Not Sufficient** when the answer **could be Yes or No**.

	Sufficient	Not Sufficient
Value	**1 Value**	**More than 1 Value**
Yes/No	**1 Answer (Yes or No)**	**More than 1 Answer (Yes AND No)**

Step 3: Decide *exactly* what the question is asking.

To properly evaluate the statements, you must have a very precise understanding of the question asked in the question stem. Ask yourself two questions:

1. What, *precisely*, would be *sufficient*?
2. What, *precisely*, would *not* be *sufficient*?

For instance, suppose the question is, "What is *x*?"

1. What, precisely, would be sufficient? **One value for *x*** (e.g., *x* = 5).
2. What, precisely, would not be sufficient? **More than one value for *x*** (e.g., *x* is prime).

Step 4: Use the Grid to evaluate the statements.

The answer choices need to be evaluated in the proper order. The Grid is a simple but effective tool to help you keep track of your progress. Write the following on your page:

AD
BCE

The two columns below will tell you how to work through the Grid:

First, **evaluate Statement (1).**

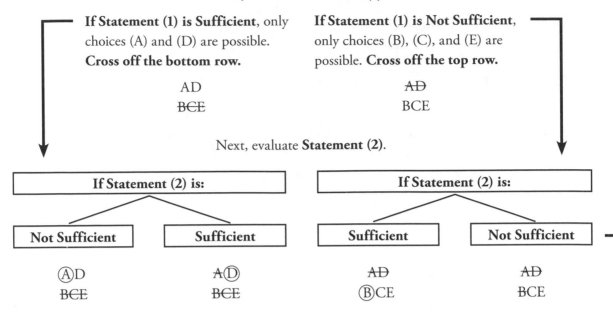

If Statement (1) is Sufficient, only choices (A) and (D) are possible. **Cross off the bottom row.**

If Statement (1) is Not Sufficient, only choices (B), (C), and (E) are possible. **Cross off the top row.**

Next, evaluate **Statement (2).**

Notice that the first two steps are always the same: evaluate Statement (1) then evaluate Statement (2).

If neither Statement by itself is sufficient, then the only two possible answers are (C) and (E). The next step is to look at the Statements TOGETHER:

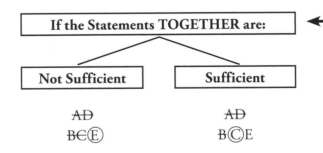

Putting It All Together

Now that you know the process, it's time to work through the practice problem start to finish.

> Jon's birthday party is this week. What day of the week is the party on?
>
>> (1) The party is not on Monday or Tuesday.
>> (2) The party is not on Wednesday, Thursday, or Friday.
>
> (A) Statement (1) ALONE is sufficient, but statement (2) is NOT sufficient
> (B) Statement (2) ALONE is sufficient, but statement (1) is NOT sufficient
> (C) BOTH statements TOGETHER are sufficient, but NEITHER statement ALONE is sufficient
> (D) EACH statement ALONE is sufficient
> (E) Statements (1) and (2) TOGETHER are NOT sufficient

Step 1: Separate *additional info* from the *actual question*.

Question	Additional Info
What day of the week is the party on?	Jon's birthday party is this week.

Step 2: Determine whether the question is Value or Yes/No.

You need to know the exact day of the week that the party is on.

This is a Value question.

Step 3: Decide *exactly* what the question is asking.

What, precisely, would be sufficient? **One possible day of the week.**
What, precisely, would not be sufficient? **More than one possible day of the week.**

Step 4: Use the Grid to evaluate the statements.

Evaluate Statement (1): Statement (1) tells you that the party is *not* on Monday or Tuesday. The party could still be on Wednesday, Thursday, Friday, Saturday, or Sunday. Statement (1) is Not Sufficient.

~~AD~~
BCE

Evaluate Statement (2): Statement (2) tells you that the party is *not* on Wednesday, Thursday, or Friday. The party could still be on Saturday, Sunday, Monday, or Tuesday. Statement (2) is Not Sufficient.

~~AD~~
~~BCE~~

Now that you've verified neither statement is sufficient on its own, it's time to evaluate the statements taken together.

Evaluate (1) AND (2): Taking both statements together, we know the party is not on Monday, Tuesday, Wednesday, Thursday, or Friday. The party could still be on Saturday or Sunday. Statements (1) and (2) together are Not Sufficient.

~~AD~~
~~BC~~(E)

The correct answer is **(E)**.

Putting It All Together (Again)

Now try a different, but related, question:

> It rains all day every Saturday and Sunday in Seattle, and never on any other day.
> Is it raining in Seattle right now?
>
> (1) Today is not Monday or Tuesday.
> (2) Today is not Wednesday, Thursday, or Friday.

(A) Statement (1) ALONE is sufficient, but statement (2) is NOT sufficient
(B) Statement (2) ALONE is sufficient, but statement (1) is NOT sufficient
(C) BOTH statements TOGETHER are sufficient, but NEITHER statement ALONE is sufficient
(D) EACH statement ALONE is sufficient
(E) Statements (1) and (2) TOGETHER are NOT sufficient

The statements are exactly the same as in the previous example, but the question has changed. The process is still the same.

Step 1: Separate *additional info* from the *actual question*.

Question	Additional Info
Is it raining in Seattle right now?	It rains all day every Saturday and Sunday in Seattle, and never on any other day.

Step 2: Determine whether the question is Value or Yes/No.

There are two possible answers to this question:

1. Yes, it is raining in Seattle right now.
2. No, it is not raining in Seattle right now.

This is a Yes/No question.

Step 3: Decide *exactly* what the question is asking.

Be careful. This part of the process is usually more complicated when the question is Yes/No. Sufficient is defined as providing a definite answer to the Yes/No question. Since the statements often allow for multiple possible values, you have to ask the Yes/No question for all the possible values.

Before you look at the statements, keep in mind there are only 7 days of the week. You know the answer to the question on each of those days as well. If today is Saturday or Sunday, the answer is **yes, it is raining in Seattle right now**. If today is Monday, Tuesday, Wednesday, Thursday, or Friday, the answer is **no, it is not raining in Seattle right now**.

What, precisely, would be sufficient? **It is definitely raining (Saturday or Sunday) OR it is definitely NOT raining (Monday through Friday).**
What, precisely, would not be sufficient? **It may be raining (e.g., Today is either Friday or Saturday).**

Step 4: Use the Grid to evaluate the statements.

Evaluate Statement (1): Statement (1) tells you that today is *not* Monday or Tuesday. Today could still be Wednesday, Thursday, Friday, Saturday, or Sunday. It might be raining in Seattle right now. You cannot know for sure. Statement (1) is Not Sufficient.

~~AD~~
BCE

Evaluate Statement (2): Statement (2) tells you that today is *not* Wednesday, Thursday, or Friday. Today could still be Saturday, Sunday, Monday, or Tuesday. It might be raining in Seattle right now. You cannot know for sure. Statement (2) is Not Sufficient.

~~AD~~
~~B~~CE

Now that you've verified neither statement is sufficient on its own, it's time to evaluate the statement taken together.

Evaluate (1) AND (2): Taking both statements together, you know that today is not Monday, Tuesday, Wednesday, Thursday, or Friday. Today could still be on Saturday or Sunday. If today is Saturday, you know that it is raining in Seattle. If today is Sunday, you know that it is raining in Seattle. Either way, you can say definitely that **yes, it is raining in Seattle right now**. Taken together, Statements (1) and (2) are Sufficient.

~~AD~~
BⒸE

The correct answer is **(C)**.

Weighted Averages on Data Sufficiency

Data Sufficiency questions that involve weighted averages can always be answered by translating words into equations and solving for the desired values. The questions in this section are no exception. However, the focus here will be on explanations that make use of a conceptual understanding of weighted averages, and will largely avoid equations.

Consider this problem:

> The average number of students per class at School X is 25 and the average number of students per class at School Y is 33. Is the average number of students per class for both schools combined less than 29 ?
>
> (1) There are 12 classes in School X.
> (2) There are more classes in School X than in School Y.

In this question, the data points are the average numbers of students per class (25 in School X and 33 in School Y). Notice that 29 is exactly halfway between 25 and 33. If there are an equal number of classes in both schools, then the average number of students per class will be exactly 29.

The question asks if the average number of students per class is less than 29. If there are more classes in School X, the average will be closer to 25 than to 33, and less than 29. This question is really asking if there are more classes in School X than in School Y.

Statement 1 only tells you how many classes there are in School X. This information by itself does not help you. Cross off A and D on your grid.

Notice that Statement 2 actually tells you exactly what you need to know. If there are more classes in School X, then the average number of students per class will be less than 29. The statement is sufficient, so the correct answer is (B).

Now try a tougher example:

> Tickets to a play cost $10 for children and $25 for adults. If 100 tickets were sold, were more adult tickets sold than children's tickets?
>
> (1) The average revenue per ticket was $18.
> (2) The revenue from ticket sales exceeded $1,750.

First things first: how would you recognize that this question is about weighted averages? The two different prices for tickets are like two different data points, and the number of tickets sold will act as the weight.

You can use weighted averages to work through the statements. Statement 1 should seem pretty familiar by now: $18 is closer to $25 than to $10. That means that there must have been more adult tickets sold than children's tickets. Statement 1 is sufficient. Cross off B, C, and E on your grid.

Now look at Statement 2. Statement 2 says that the total revenue from ticket sales exceeded $1,750. Where did that number come from?

To figure that out, look at the information in the question stem again. Notice that the question actually told you that 100 tickets were sold. Consider two extreme scenarios:

> 100 children's tickets sold = 100 × $10 = $1,000 revenue
> 100 adult tickets sold = 100 × $25 = $2,500 revenue

If there were an equal number of adult and children's tickets sold, the revenue would be exactly in the middle: $1,750. That's the connection to weighted averages. If the revenue is greater than $1,750, it is closer to $2,500 than to $1,000, which means more adult tickets must have been sold. Statement 2 is also sufficient. The correct answer is (D).

Although questions that involve weighted averages can always be solved algebraically, a good conceptual understanding of weighted averages will allow you to avoid a lot of computation while still answering questions correctly.

Replacing Variables with Numbers

Which of the following questions is easier to answer?

How many miles can a car going x miles per hour travel in y hours?	How many miles can a car going 40 miles per hour travel in 3 hours?
(A) $\dfrac{x}{y}$ (B) $\dfrac{y}{x}$ (C) xy	(A) $\dfrac{40}{3}$ (B) $\dfrac{3}{40}$ (C) 120

Most likely, you found the question on the right easier. In general, numbers are easier to work with than variables.

Notice that the questions are actually identical, except for the fact that x has been replaced by 40, and y has been replaced by 3. In both questions, the relevant formula is $D = RT$.

$$x \, \frac{\text{miles}}{\text{hour}} \times y \text{ hours} = xy \text{ miles}$$

$$40 \, \frac{\text{miles}}{\text{hour}} \times 3 \text{ hours} = 120 \text{ miles}$$

Problems that have **variables in the answer choices** can almost always be answered by **replacing variables with numbers**.

There are three basic steps:

Step 1: Identify unknowns and replace them with numbers.

In the above example, you replaced *x* with 40 and replaced *y* with 3.

Step 2: Use these numbers to calculate the answer to the problem.

A car traveling 40 miles per hour for 3 hours travels 120 miles. Remember the number you calculate in this step. You should refer to this as the target.

Step 3: Plug the same numbers into the answer choices.

The correct answer will be equal to the target number.

Notice that the answers to the problem on the right are in the same form as the answers to the problem on the left. All *x*'s have been replaced with 40's and all *y*'s have been replaced with 3's.

The correct answer is (C), because it equals 120, which is the same number we calculated in Step 2.

This technique can also be used with more complicated word problems. For example:

A park ranger travels from his base to a campsite via truck at *r* miles per hour. Upon arriving, he collects a snowmobile and uses it to return to base. If the camp site is *d* miles from the park ranger's base and the entire trip took *t* hours to complete, what was his speed on the snowmobile, in terms of *t*, *d*, and *r*?

(A) $tr - d$
(B) $td - r$
(C) $\dfrac{dr}{rt - d}$
(D) $\dfrac{drt}{dt - r}$
(E) $\dfrac{td - r}{d}$

The key to replacing variables with numbers is to pick numbers that make calculation easy. You should pick the rate and the distance so that the time traveled is an integer. You also want to pick numbers that are small enough that they will be easy to plug in to the answer choices.

Say that *r* = 10 and *d* = 20. That way it takes 2 hours for the ranger to reach the camp. To keep things easy, you can say that the whole trip took 4 hours. That would mean that the ranger traveled 10 miles per hour on the snowmobile as well.

You've picked numbers for your variables and calculated a target:

$$r = 10 \qquad d = 20 \qquad t = 4$$

Target $= 10$

Now you need to figure out which answer choice matches the target:

(A) $tr - d = (4)(10) - (20) = 20$

(B) $td - r = (4)(20) - (10) = 70$

(C) $\dfrac{dr}{rt - d} = \dfrac{(20)(10)}{(10)(4) - (20)} = \dfrac{200}{20} = 10$

(D) $\dfrac{drt}{dt - r} = \dfrac{(20)(10)(4)}{(20)(4) - (10)} = \dfrac{800}{70}$

(E) $\dfrac{td - r}{d} = \dfrac{(4)(20) - (10)}{20} = \dfrac{70}{20}$

The correct answer is (C).

Backsolving

The standard way to solve word problems is to translate the words into equations, and solve for the desired value. Some word problems, however, contain equations that make the desired value difficult to solve for.

There is an alternate method that can help avoid some of the work. Instead of solving for the desired value, you can test the answer choices and see which one makes the equations true. For example:

> Preeti has money in two separate bank accounts. Account X earns 8% interest annually and account Y earns 15% interest annually. Preeti earned a total of $53 in interest last year. If the total amount of money in the accounts at the beginning of last year was $400, and there were no other deposits or withdrawals, how much money was in account Y?
>
> (A) $100   (B) $150   (C) $200   (D) $250   (E) $300

Let x be the total amount of money in account X and let y be the total amount of money in account Y. The question provides you with enough information to create two equations:

$$x + y = 400 \qquad 0.08x + 0.15y = 53$$

You need to solve for y, but doing so may be time-consuming and equations involving decimals can get quite messy. Instead, you can test answer choices. This technique is called **backsolving**.

With backsolving, you will start by assuming the value of y. If the correct answer were (C), y would be 200. You can use the first equation to find the value of x. Then, you will plug x and y into the second equation. If it is true, you know you have the correct answer.

If $y = 200$, $x = 200$ (because $x + y = 400$). Plug $x = 200$ and $y = 200$ into the second equation:

$$0.08(200) + 0.15(200) = 53$$
$$16 + 30 = 53$$
$$46 \neq 53$$

Answer choice (C) is incorrect. If that were all you knew, this technique would be quite tedious. But you can actually eliminate two other answer choices. The answer was incorrect because 8 percent of x and 15 percent of y only added up to 46, not 53. You need an answer choice that will make that sum larger.

Backsolving typically works best when you test answer choice (C) first, as it will allow you to eliminate three answer choices (if (C) is wrong). If, in contrast, you tested answer choice (A) first and it was wrong, you would only be able to eliminate (A).

Account Y earns a higher interest rate than account X, so if you make y larger and x smaller, the sum should be larger. You can also cross off answer choices A and B.

Now that you know the answer is either (D) or (E), you need to do the math only one more time. If the answer choice you choose to test works, you know that's the answer. If it doesn't work, you know the other answer choice must be correct.

Looking at the answer choices, it actually looks like (E) would be easier to test. The numbers 300 and 100 will be easier to use than 250 and 150.

If you assume that $y = 300$, then x must equal 100. Plug these values into the second equation:

$$0.08(100) + 0.15(300) = 53$$
$$8 + 45 = 53$$
$$53 = 53$$

The equation is true, so answer choice (E) is correct.

Backsolving can be a time-saving technique because, at most, you will need to test two answer choices. Test answer choice (C) first to really save time. Although backsolving does not allow you to avoid algebra entirely, it can be useful when it seems that solving for the desired value will involve messy equations.

Using Charts to Organize Variables

When a word problem involves several quantities and multiple relationships, a chart or table can be used to effectively organize the information.

Let's revisit problem #7 from the Chapter 1 problem set:

> A circus earned $150,000 in ticket revenue by selling 1,800 V.I.P. and Standard tickets. They sold 25% more Standard tickets than V.I.P. tickets. If the revenue from Standard tickets represents one-third of the total ticket revenue, what is the price of a V.I.P. ticket?

If you haven't already done so, take a moment to answer this question.

In this problem, there are several unknowns: the number of Standard and V.I.P tickets, the cost per ticket for each type of ticket, revenue generated, etc. Trying to create a variable for each of these values could be quite tedious and confusing.

One way to deal with all these unknowns is to create a table. The relationship (Price) × (Quantity) = (Revenue) is relevant for both Standard and V.I.P. tickets:

	Price per Ticket × ($ / ticket)	Quantity (# of tickets)	=	Revenue ($)
Standard				
V.I.P				

But even this chart does not actually keep track of all the relationships in the problem. You also know that the number of Standard tickets plus the number of V.I.P. tickets equals the total number of tickets. Similarly, the revenues from each type of ticket sum to the total revenue generated from tickets. You should add a third row to the chart:

	Price per Ticket × ($ / ticket)	Quantity (# of tickets)	=	Revenue ($)
Standard				
V.I.P				
Total	—			

Notice that you've used this strategy before; charts are useful on rate problems and overlapping-sets problems. You have a similar advantage here: the chart allows you to keep track of a number of different relationships all at the same time.

Now you can enter information into the chart. You know that the total revenue is $150,000, and the to-tal number of tickets sold is 1,800. You also know that the circus sold 25% more Standard tickets than

V.I.P. tickets. If you let x equal the number of V.I.P. tickets sold, then the number of Standard tickets sold is $1.25x$:

	Price per Ticket × ($ / ticket)	Quantity = (# of tickets)	Revenue ($)
Standard		$1.25x$	
V.I.P		x	
Total	—	1,800	150,000

The revenue from Standard tickets is one-third the total revenue, which is $150,000. So the revenue from Standard tickets is $50,000 and the revenue from V.I.P. tickets is $100,000. Additionally, you now have an equation for the number of tickets:

$$1.25x + x = 1,800$$
$$2,25x = 1,800$$
$$x = 800$$

800 V.I.P. tickets were sold, and 1,000 Standard tickets were sold:

	Price per Ticket × ($ / ticket)	Quantity = (# of tickets)	Revenue ($)
Standard		1,000	50,000
V.I.P		800	100,000
Total	—	1,800	150,000

Now, at last, you can solve for the price of a V.I.P. ticket. Price per ticket times the number of tickets equals the revenue:

$$p \times 800 = 100,000$$
$$p = 125$$

The price of a V.I.P. ticket is $125.

A chart was useful for this problem because of the number of relationships present in the argument. Instead of writing down a lot of equations, you could organize the information in a chart.

Problem Set

1. A car travels from Town A to Town B at an average speed of 40 miles per hour, and returns immediately along the same route at an average speed of 50 miles per hour. What is the average speed in miles per hour for the round-trip?

2. Two racecar drivers, Abernathy and Berdoff, are driving around a circular track. If Abernathy is 200 meters behind Berdoff and both drivers drive at their respective constant rates, how long, in seconds, will it take for Abernathy to catch up to Berdoff?

    (1) The circumference of the racetrack is 1,400 meters.
    (2) Abernathy is driving 25 meters per minute faster than Berdoff.

3. a, b, and c are integers in the set $\{a, b, c, 51, 85, 72\}$. Is the median of the set greater than 70?

    (1) $b > c > 69$
    (2) $a < c < 71$

4. A list kept at Town Hall contains the town's average daily temperature in Fahrenheit, rounded to the nearest integer. A particular completed month has either 30 or 31 days. How many days does the month have?

    (1) The median temperature is 73.5.
    (2) The sum of the average daily temperatures is divisible by 3.

5. A store sells chairs and tables. If the price of 3 chairs and 1 table is 60% of the price of 1 chair and 3 tables, and the price of 1 table and 1 chair is $60, what is the price, in dollars, of 1 table? (Assume that every chair has the same price and every table has the same price.)

    (A) 15   (B) 20   (C) 30   (D) 40   (E) 45

6. Boys and girls in a class are writing letters. There are twice as many girls as boys in the class, and each girl writes 3 more letters than each boy. If boys write 24 of the 90 total letters written by the class, how many letters does each boy write?

Solutions

1. $44\frac{4}{9}$: Use a Multiple RTD chart to solve this problem. Start by selecting a Smart Number for d: 200 miles. (This is a common multiple of the two rates in the problem.) Then, work backwards to find the time for each trip and the total time:

	R (mi/hr)	×	T (hr)	=	D (mi)
A to B	40	×	t_1	=	200
B to A	50	×	t_2	=	200
Total	—		t		400

$$t_1 = \frac{200}{40} = 5 \text{ hrs} \qquad t_2 = \frac{200}{50} = 4 \text{ hrs} \qquad t = 4 + 5 = 9 \text{ hours}$$

The average speed $= \dfrac{\text{total distance}}{\text{total time}} = \dfrac{400}{9} = 44\frac{4}{9}$ miles per hour.

Do NOT simply average 40 miles per hour and 50 miles per hour to get 45 miles per hour. The fact that the right answer is very close to this wrong result makes this error especially pernicious: avoid it at all costs!

2. **(B):** This question is much easier than most people assume on first glance! It doesn't matter that the track is circular—if one driver is 200 meters behind another driver and both drive at constant rates, all you need to know in order to determine the time it takes for the rear driver to catch up is the rate at which the rear driver is "gaining" on the front driver.

While of course having the two drivers' individual rates would be nice, you don't actually even need that much information—all you need is the rate at which Abernathy is catching up. (When drivers are traveling in the same direction, you subtract their rates; you only need this relative rate.)

Thus, the rephrase is, "What is the difference in the two drivers' rates?"

(1) INSUFFICIENT: Knowing the length of the track is insufficient and actually pretty useless, since your math problem really ends at the point that Abernathy catches up to Berdoff. Who cares how much track is in front of them when that happens?

(2) SUFFICIENT: This is exactly what you need—if Abernathy is "gaining" at 25 meters per minute, then it will take him 8 minutes to catch up (time = distance/rate, so time = 200/25, which is equal to 8).

The answer is (B).

3. **(A):** The median of a set of six integers is the average of the two middle terms (the 3rd and 4th) when the terms are placed in order from low to high.

(1) SUFFICIENT: Look at the minimum case. If c is an integer greater than 69, the smallest c can be is 70. By similar logic, the smallest b could be is 71. In this case, the set is {51, 70, 71, 72, 85, a}. The only unknown is the value of a:

If $a \leq 51$, the ordered set is {a, 51, 70, 71, 72, 85}; median = (70 + 71)/2 = 70.5.
If $51 < a \leq 70$, the ordered set is {51, a, 70, 71, 72, 85}; median = (70 + 71)/2 = 70.5.
If $a = 71$, the ordered set is {51, 70, a, 71, 72, 85}; median = (71 + 71)/2 = 71.
If $a = 72$, the ordered set is {51, 70, 71, 72, a, 85}; median = (71 + 72)/2 = 71.5.
If $a > 72$, the order of the first four terms doesn't change from the line above, so median = 71.5.

In all cases, the median is greater than 70, so the answer is a definite "yes."

Furthermore, if c and b are larger than the minimum case you tested, say $c = 71$ and $b = 72$ or $c = 100$ and $b = 150$, a quick check reveals that there is no a value that would make the median ≤ 70.

(2) INSUFFICIENT: Look at the maximum case. If c is an integer less than 71, the greatest c can be is 70. By similar logic, the greatest a could be is 69. In this case, the set is {b, 51, 69, 70, 72, 85}. The only unknown is the value of b:

If $b \leq 51$, the ordered set is {b, 51, 69, 70, 72, 85}; median = (69 + 70)/2 = 69.5.
If $b = 70$, the ordered set is {51, 69, 70, 70, 72, 85}; median = (70 + 70)/2 = 70.
If $b = 71$, the ordered set is {51, 69, 70, 71, 72, 85}; median = (70 + 71)/2 = 70.5.

In some cases, the median is greater than 70, but in other cases, it isn't. The answer is "maybe."

The correct answer is (A).

4. **(A):** This question is really about evens and odds. A list of values contains either 30 or 31 elements. Does the list have an even or an odd number of elements?

(1) SUFFICIENT: Since every item in the list is an integer, the only way for the median to be a non-integer is if there is an even number of items in the list (and therefore no middle term—in this case, the median is calculated as the average of the two middle terms). Therefore, the month must have an even number of days, so it must contain 30 days.

(2) INSUFFICIENT: The sum of either 30 or 31 values is divisible by 3. Since there are no constraints on what the temperatures might be, it is perfectly possible to have a list of 30 values or a list of 31 values that add up to a multiple of 3. For example, if the temperature every day were 60 degrees, the sum of the temperatures would be divisible by 3 no matter how many days the month contained.

The correct answer is (A).

5. **(E) 45:** First, let c equal the price of a chair and let t equal the price of a table. You can create two equations from the information provided in the question:

the price of 3 chairs and 1 table is 60% of the price of 1 chair and 3 tables → $3c + t = 0.6(c + 3t)$
the price of 1 table and 1 chair is $60 → $c + t = 60$

At this point, you have two good methods available to solve for t. You can use substitution, or you can backsolve from the answer choices.

A little intuition about the answer choices can make backsolving very efficient on this problem. First, notice that answer choice (C) does not make sense as an answer. If 1 table costs $30, then 1 chair also costs $30 (because $c + t = 60$). But if that was the case, then the price of 3 chairs and 1 table would equal the cost of 1 chair and 3 tables. You can eliminate answer choice (C).

Next you need to figure out if the price of 1 table should be higher or lower than $30. If it is cheaper to buy 3 chairs and 1 table than it is to buy 1 chair and 3 tables, then it must be true that tables are more expensive than chairs. You can also eliminate answer choices (A) and (B).

Now try backsolving with answer choice (D). If the price of 1 table is $40, then the price of 1 chair is $20. You can plug these values into the first equation:

$$3c + t = 0.6(c + 3t)$$
$$3(20) + (40) = 0.6((20) + 3(40))$$
$$100 = 0.6(140)$$
$$100 = 84$$

This equation does not hold true, which means answer choice (D) is wrong. You could confidently pick answer choice (E) at this point. If you want to prove (E) is right, you can do the calculation. If 1 table costs $45, then 1 chair costs $15:

$$3c + t = 0.6(c + 3t)$$
$$3(15) + (45) = 0.6((15) + 3(45))$$
$$90 = 0.6(150)$$
$$90 = 90$$

The equation is true, so answer choice (E) is correct.

Alternatively, you could have used substitution. Isolate c in the second equation:

$$c + t = 60$$
$$c = t - 60$$

Now replace c with $(60 - t)$ in the first equation:

$$3c + t = 0.6(c + 3t)$$
$$3(60 - t) + t = 0.6((60 - t) + 3t)$$
$$180 - 3t + t = 0.6(60 + 2t)$$
$$180 - 2t = 36 + 1.2t$$
$$144 = 3.2t$$
$$45 = t$$

6. 8: There are a lot of relationships presented in this question. You should set up a chart to keep track of all the information.

	# of Children	×	Letters / Child	=	# of Letters Written
Girls					
Boys					

There are twice as many girls as boys. If b is the number of boys in the class, then $2b$ is the number of girls. Similarly, if every boy writes x letters, then every girl writes $(x + 3)$ letters:

	# of Children	×	Letters / Child	=	# of Letters Written
Girls	$2b$		$x + 3$		$2bx + 6b$
Boys	b		x		bx

You also know that the boys wrote 24 letters, which means that girls wrote $90 - 24 = 66$ letters:

	# of children	×	Letters / child	=	# of letters written
Girls	$2b$		$x + 3$		$2bx + 6b = 66$
Boys	b		x		$bx = 24$

You ultimately need to solve for x. In the meantime, you can use the fact that $bx = 24$ to simplify the equation for the total number of letters written by girls:

$$2bx + 6b = 66$$
$$2(24) + 6b = 66$$
$$48 + 6b = 66$$
$$6b = 18$$
$$b = 3$$

If $b = 3$, and $bx = 24$, then $x = 8$. Each boy wrote 8 letters.

Chapter 7
of
Word Problems

Extra Problem Types

In This Chapter. . .

Chapter 7:

Extra Problem Types

The GMAT occasionally contains problems that fall under one of three umbrellas:

1. **Optimization:** maximizing or minimizing a quantity by choosing optimal values of related quantities.
2. **Grouping:** putting people or items into different groups to maximize or minimize some characteristic.
3. **Scheduling:** planning a timeline to coordinate events according to a set of restrictions.

You should approach all three of these problem types with the same general outlook, although it is unlikely that you will see more than one of them on the same administration of the GMAT. The general approach is to focus on **extreme scenarios**.

You should mind the following three considerations when considering any grouping, scheduling, or optimization problem:

1. Be aware of both ***explicit constraints*** (restrictions actually stated in the text) and ***hidden constraints*** (restrictions implied by the real-world aspects of a problem). For instance, in a problem requiring the separation of 40 people into 6 groups, hidden constraints require the number of people in each group to be a positive whole number.
2. In most cases, you can maximize or minimize quantities (or optimize schedules, etc.) by ***choosing the highest or lowest values*** of the variables that you are allowed to select.
3. Be very careful about ***rounding***. Some problems may require you to round up, others down, and still others not at all.

Optimization

In general optimization problems, you are asked to maximize or minimize some quantity, given constraints on other quantities. These quantities are all related through some equation.

Consider the following problem:

> The guests at a football banquet consumed a total of 401 pounds of food. If no individual guest consumed more than 2.5 pounds of food, what is the minimum number of guests that could have attended the banquet?

You can visualize the underlying equation in the following table:

Pounds of Food per Guest	×	Guests	=	Total Pounds of Food
At MOST 2.5 Maximize	×	At LEAST ??? Minimize	=	EXACTLY 401 Constant

Notice that finding the minimum value of the number of guests involves using the maximum pounds of food per guest, because the two quantities multiply to a constant. This sort of inversion is typical.

Begin by considering the extreme case in which each guest eats as much food as possible, or 2.5 pounds apiece. The corresponding number of guests at the banquet works out to 401/2.5 = 160.4 people.

However, you obviously cannot have a fractional number of guests at the banquet. Thus, the answer must be rounded. To determine whether to round up or down, consider the explicit constraint: the amount of food per guest is a maximum of 2.5 pounds per guest. Therefore, the minimum number of guests is 160.4 (if guests could be fractional), and you must round up to make the number of guests an integer: 161.

Note the careful reasoning required! Although the phrase "minimum number of guests" may tempt you to round down, you will get an incorrect answer if you do so. In general, as you solve this sort of problem, put the extreme case into the underlying equation, and solve. Then round appropriately.

Grouping

In grouping problems, you make complete groups of items, drawing these items out of a larger pool. The goal is to maximize or minimize some quantity, such as the number of complete groups or the number of leftover items that do not fit into complete groups. As such, these problems are really a special case of optimization. One approach is to determine the limiting factor on the number of complete groups. That is, if you need different types of items for a complete group, figure out how many groups you can make with each item, ignoring the other types (as if you had unlimited quantities of those other items). Then compare your results. Consider the following example:

> Orange Computers is breaking up its conference attendees into groups. Each group must have exactly one person from Division A, two people from Division B, and three people from Division C. There are 20 people from Division A, 30 people from Division B, and 40 people from Division C at the conference. What is the smallest number of people who will not be able to be assigned to a group?

The first step is to find out how many groups you can make with the people from each division separately, ignoring the other divisions. There are enough Division A people for 20 groups, but only enough Division B people for 15 groups (= 30 people ÷ 2 people per group). As for Division C, there are only enough people for 13 groups, since 40 people ÷ 3 people per group = 13 groups, plus one person left over. So the limiting factor is Division C: only 13 complete groups can be formed. These 13 groups will take up 13 Division A people (leaving 20 − 13 = 7 left over) and 26 Division B people (leaving 30 − 26 = 4 left over). Together with the 1 Division C person left over, 1 + 4 + 7 = 12 people will be left over in total.

For some grouping problems, you may want to think about the most or least evenly distributed arrangements of the items. That is, assign items to groups as evenly (or unevenly) as possible to create extreme cases.

Scheduling

Scheduling problems, which require you to determine possible schedules satisfying a variety of constraints, can usually be tackled by careful consideration of **extreme possibilities**, usually the earliest and latest possible time slots for the events to be scheduled. Consider the following problem:

> How many days after the purchase of Product X does its standard warranty expire? (1997 is not a leap year.)
>
> (1)   When Mark purchased Product X in January 1997, the warranty did not expire until March 1997.
> (2)   When Santos purchased Product X in May 1997, the warranty expired in May 1997.

Rephrase the two statements in terms of extreme possibilities:

> (1)   Shortest possible warranty period: Jan. 31 to Mar. 1 (29 days later)
>   Longest possible warranty period: Jan. 1 to Mar. 31 (89 days later)
>   Note that 1997 was not a leap year.
> (2)   Shortest possible warranty period: May 1 to May 2, or similar (1 day later)
>   Longest possible warranty period: May 1 to May 31 (30 days later)

Even taking both statements together, there are still two possibilities—29 days and 30 days —so both statements together are still insufficient.

Note that, had the given year been a leap year, the two statements together would have become sufficient! Moral of the story: *Read the problem very, very carefully.*

Computation Problems

Very occasionally, the GMAT features problems centered on computation—problems that contain no variables at all, and in principle require nothing more than "plug and chug" techniques. Sometimes, however, these problems compensate for the lack of variables with correspondingly more difficult or obscure calculations. Most of them can be tackled with the following strategies:

- Take careful ***inventory*** of any and all quantities presented in the problem. Be sure to pay attention to both *numbers and units*, as the interplay between the units of different quantities may give away the correct way to relate them.
- Use the same techniques and equations that have been developed for other types of problems (especially work/rate, percent, and profit problems). If the arithmetic is complicated enough, you might want to designate variables.
- Draw a diagram, table, or chart to organize information, if necessary.
- ***Read the problem carefully***, as purely computation-based problems tend to be trickier than other problems!

Here is an example:

> Five identical pieces of wire are soldered together to form a longer wire, with the
> pieces overlapping by 4 cm at each join. If the wire thus made is exactly 1 meter
> long, how long is each of the identical pieces? (1 meter = 100 cm)

A diagram is helpful for this problem. Note that without a diagram it is easy to assume that, because there are five pieces, there must be five joins. Instead, there are only four joins:

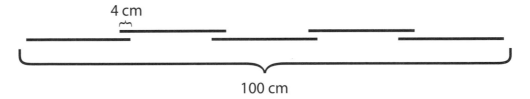

4 cm

100 cm

First, convert to make compatible units: 1 meter = 100 cm.

Each join includes 4 cm of *both* wires joined, but is only counted once in the total length of 100 cm. Therefore, the total length of *all* the original wires is 100 + 4(4) = 116 cm. Because there are five wires, each wire is 116/5 = 23.2 cm long. (If you prefer, you could set this problem up with a variable: $5x - 16 = 100$.)

On **Data Sufficiency** problems involving computation, remember that there is no need to perform computations! If you can simply establish that you have enough information to compute the answer to a problem, you have your answer ("sufficient").

Graphing Problems

Very occasionally, the GMAT will ask you to interpret a graph, table, or chart. These problems feature considerable variety, but in most cases the following tips can be helpful:

- Study the graph or table carefully *both before and after* reading the problem. When you examine the graph, pay special attention to *labels, units, and scales*.
- Look for *patterns* in the shape of graphs (or in the numbers in tables). Typical patterns include increasing values, decreasing values, and conspicuous maximum or minimum values.

Problem Set

1. Velma has exactly one week to learn all 71 Japanese hiragana characters. If she can learn at most a dozen of them on any one day and will only have time to learn four of them on Friday, what is the least number of hiragana that Velma will have to learn on Saturday?

2. When it is 2:01pm Sunday afternoon in Nullepart, it is Monday in Eimissaan. When it is 1:00pm Wednesday in Eimissaan, it is also Wednesday in Nullepart. When it is noon Friday in Nullepart, what is the possible range of times in Eimissaan?

3. Huey's Hip Pizza sells two sizes of square pizzas: a small pizza that measures 10 inches on a side and costs $10, and a large pizza that measures 15 inches on a side and costs $20. If two friends go to Huey's with $30 apiece, how many more square inches of pizza can they buy if they pool their money than if they each purchase pizza alone?

4. An eccentric casino owner decides that his casino should only use chips in $5 and $7 denominations. Which of the following amounts cannot be paid out using these chips?

    $31 $29 $26 $23 $21

5. A "Collector's Coin Set" contains a one dollar coin, a fifty-cent coin, a quarter (= 25 cents), a dime (= 10 cents), a nickel (= 5 cents), and a penny (= 1 cent). The Coin Sets are sold for the combined face price of the currency. If Colin buys as many Coin Sets as he can with the $25 he has, how much change will Colin have left over?

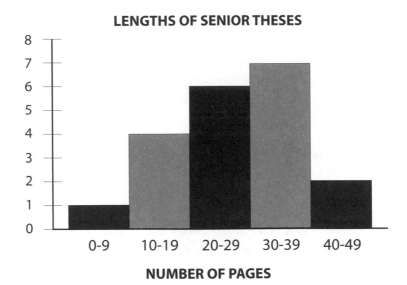

6. Each senior in a college course wrote a thesis. The lengths, in pages, of those seniors'
    theses are summarized in the graph above.

    a. What is the *least* possible number of seniors whose theses were within six
        pages of the median length?

    b. What is the *greatest* possible number of seniors whose theses were within six
        pages of the median length?

P

Solutions

1. **7:** To minimize the number of hiragana that Velma will have to learn on Saturday, consider the extreme case in which she learns *as many* hiragana *as possible* on the other days. She learns 4 on Friday, leaving $71 - 4 = 67$ for the other six days of the week. If Velma learns the maximum of 12 hiragana on the other five days (besides Saturday), then she will have $67 - 5(12) = 7$ left for Saturday.

2. **Anywhere from 10pm Friday to 1am Saturday:** The first statement tells you that the time in Eimissaan is at least 10 hours ahead of the time in Nullepart; given this information, the second statement tells you that the time in Eimissaan is at most 13 hours ahead of the time in Nullepart. (The second statement *by itself* could allow Nullepart time to be ahead of Eimissaan time, but that situation is already precluded by the first statement.) Therefore, the time in Eimissaan is between 10 and 13 hours ahead of the time in Nullepart.

3. **25 square inches:** First, figure the area of each pizza: the small is 100 square inches, and the large is 225 square inches. If the two friends pool their money, they can buy three large pizzas, which have a total area of 675 square inches. If they buy individually, though, then each friend will have to buy one large pizza and one small pizza, so they will only have a total of $2(100 + 225) = 650$ square inches of pizza.

4. **(D):** This problem is similar to a Scheduling problem in which you have a number of 5-hour and 7-hour tasks, and your mission is to figure out what total amount of time would be impossible to take. Either way, you have some integer number of 5's and some integer number of 7's. Which of the answer choices cannot be the sum? One efficient way to eliminate choices is first to cross off any multiples of 7 and/or 5, which eliminates (E). Now, any other possible sums must have at least one 5 and one 7 in them. So you can subtract off 5's one at a time until you reach a multiple of 7. (It is easier to subtract 5's than 7's, because our number system is base-10.) Answer choice (A): $31 - 5 = 26$; $26 - 5 = 21$, a multiple of 7; this eliminates (A). (In other words, $31 = 3 \times 7 + 2 \times 5$.) Answer choice (B): $29 - 5 = 24$; $24 - 5 = 19$; $19 - 5 = 14$, a multiple of 7; this eliminates (B). Answer choice (C): $26 - 5 = 21$, a multiple of 7; this eliminates (C). So the answer must be (D), 23. You check by successively subtracting 5 and looking for multiples of 7: $23 - 5 = 18$, not a multiple of 7; $18 - 5 = 13$, also not a multiple of 7; $13 - 5 = 8$, not a multiple of 7; and no smaller result will be a multiple of 7 either.

5. **$0.17:** The first step is to compute the value of a complete "Collector's Coin Set": $\$1.00 + \$0.50 + \$0.25 + \$0.10 + \$0.05 + \$0.01 = \$1.91$. Now, you need to divide $\$1.91$ into $\$25$. A natural first move is to multiply by 10: for $\$19.10$, Colin can buy 10 complete sets. Now add $\$1.91$ successively. Colin can buy 11 sets for $\$21.01$, 12 sets for $\$22.92$, and 13 sets for $\$24.83$. There is 17 cents left over.

6. There are twenty seniors in the class, so the median class length is the average (arithmetic mean) of the lengths of the tenth- and eleventh-longest theses, both of which are between 20 and 29 pages (inclusive). Those two theses *must* be within six pages of the median; even if they are placed as far apart as possible (20 and 29 pages), each will be only 4.5 pages away from the median.

a. **2:** Since the tenth- and eleventh-longest papers must satisfy the criterion, place them as close together as possible (to leave room to manipulate the other lengths): say 28 pages apiece. If the other four 20- to 29-page papers are each 20 or 21 pages, and all seven 30- to 39-page papers are each 35 pages or more, then only the tenth- and eleventh-longest papers are within six pages of the median.

b. **17:** If the tenth-longest paper is 25 pages and the eleventh-longest paper is 24 pages, then the median length is 24.5 pages, so all of the 20- to 29-page papers are within six pages of the median. If each of the four 10- to 19-page papers is 19 pages long and each of the seven 30- to 39-page papers is 30 pages long, then all eleven of those papers will also be within the desired range.

P

Chapter 8

of

Word Problems

Extra Consecutive Integers

In This Chapter...

Chapter 8:
Extra Consecutive Integers

Products of Consecutive Integers and Divisibility

Can you come up with a series of 3 consecutive integers in which none of the integers is a multiple of 3? Go ahead, try it! You will quickly see that any set of 3 consecutive integers must contain one multiple of 3. The result is that the product of any set of 3 consecutive integers is divisible by 3.

$$1 \times 2 \times ③ = 6 \qquad\qquad 4 \times 5 \times ⑥ = 120$$
$$2 \times ③ \times 4 = 24 \qquad\qquad 5 \times ⑥ \times 7 = 210$$
$$③ \times 4 \times 5 = 60 \qquad\qquad ⑥ \times 7 \times 8 = 336$$

According to the Factor Foundation Rule, every number is divisible by all the factors of its factors. If there is always a multiple of 3 in a set of 3 consecutive integers, the product of 3 consecutive integers will always be divisible by 3. Additionally, there will always be at least one multiple of 2 (an even number) in any set of 3 consecutive integers. Therefore, the product of 3 consecutive integers will also be divisible by 2. Thus, the product of 3 consecutive integers will always be divisible by $3! = 3 \times 2 \times 1 = 6$.

The same logic applies to a set of 4 consecutive integers, 5 consecutive integers, and any other number of consecutive integers. For instance, the product of any set of 4 consecutive integers will be divisible by $4! = 4 \times 3 \times 2 \times 1 = 24$, since that set will always contain one multiple of 4, at least one multiple of 3, and another even number (a multiple of 2).

This rule applies to any number of consecutive integers: **The product of k consecutive integers is always divisible by k factorial ($k!$).**

Sums of Consecutive Integers and Divisibility

Find the sum of any five consecutive integers:

$4 + 5 + 6 + 7 + 8 = 30$ Notice that both sums are multiples of 5.
$13 + 14 + 15 + 16 + 17 = 75$ In other words, both sums are divisible by 5.

You can generalize this observation. **For any set of consecutive integers with an ODD number of items, the sum of all the integers is ALWAYS a multiple of the number of items.** This is because the sum equals the average times the number of items. For an odd number of integers, the average is an integer, so the sum is a multiple of the number of items. The average of {13, 14, 15, 16, 17} is 15, so 15 × 5 = 13 + 14 + 15 + 16 + 17.

Find the sum of any four consecutive integers:

$1 + 2 + 3 + 4 = 10$ Notice that NEITHER sum is a multiple of 4.
$8 + 9 + 10 + 11 = 38$ In other words, both sums are NOT divisible by 4.

For any set of consecutive integers with an EVEN number of items, the sum of all the items is NEVER a multiple of the number of items. This is because the sum equals the average times the number of items. For an even number of integers, the average is never an integer, so the sum is never a multiple of the number of items. The average of {8, 9, 10, 11} is 9.5, so 9.5 × 4 = 8 + 9 + 10 + 11. That is, 8 + 9 + 10 + 11 is NOT a multiple of 4.

Consecutive Integers and Divisibility

You can use prime boxes to keep track of factors of consecutive integers. (Refer to Chapter 1 of the *Number Properties* Strategy Guide for more information on prime boxes.) Consider the following problem:

If x is an even integer, is $x(x + 1)(x + 2)$ divisible by 4?

$x(x + 1)(x + 2)$ is the product of three consecutive integers, because x is an integer. If there is one even integer in a series of consecutive integers, the product of the series is divisible by 2. If there are two even integers in a series of consecutive integers, the product of the series is divisible by 4. Set up prime boxes:

If x is even, then $x + 2$ is even, so 2 is a factor of $x(x + 1)(x + 2)$ twice. Therefore, the product $2 \times 2 = 4$ is a factor of the product of the series. The answer to the question given above is "Yes."

x	$x + 1$	$x + 1$
2		2

Problem Set

1. If r, s, and t are consecutive positive multiples of 3, is rst divisible by 27, 54, or both?

2. Is the sum of the integers from 54 to 153, inclusive, divisible by 100?

3. A machinist's salary at a factory increases by $2,000 at the end of each full year the machinist works. If the machinist's salary for the fifth year is $39,000, what is the machinist's average annual salary for his first 21 years at the factory?

4. Is the average of n consecutive integers equal to 1?

    (1) n is even.
    (2) If S is the sum of the n consecutive integers, then $0 < S < n$.

5. The product $7 \times 6 \times 5 \times 4 \times 3$ is divisible by all of the following EXCEPT:

    (A) 120   (B) 240   (C) 360   (D) 840   (E) 1,260

6. If S is a set of consecutive integers, what is the sum of the elements in S?

    (1)   The largest element in S is 55.
    (2)   There are 11 elements in S.

P

Solutions

1. **BOTH:** Because *r*, *s*, and *t* are all multiples of 3, the product *rst* must have THREE 3's as factors. Additionally, at least one of the integers must be even, so the product will have a 2 as a factor, because every other multiple of 3 is even (for example, 3, **6**, 9, **12**, etc.). $27 = 3 \times 3 \times 3$ can be constructed from the known prime factors and is therefore a factor of the product *rst*. $54 = 2 \times 3 \times 3 \times 3$ can also be constructed from the known prime factors and therefore is also factor of the product rst.

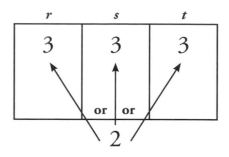

2. **NO:** There are 100 integers from 54 to 153, inclusive. For any even number of consecutive integers, the sum of all the integers is NEVER a multiple of the number of integers. Thus, the sum of the integers 54 to 153 will not be divisible by 100.

3. **$51,000:** The annual salaries of the machinist are an evenly spaced set, because each year the salary increases by the same amount. From the properties of evenly spaced sets, you know that the number you are seeking is both the median and the mean of the 21-year salary scale. It is also the average of the first and last years' salaries:

$$\text{Average Salary} = \frac{(\text{First year salary}) + (\text{Last year salary})}{2}$$

To find the salaries for the first and twenty-first years, use the fact that the salaries increase by constant increments of $2,000 per year.

The first year is four years before the fifth year, so the first year's salary is $39,000 - 4(2,000) = $31,000.

The twenty-first year is 16 years after the fifth year, so the twenty-first year salary is $39,000 + 16(2,000) = $71,000.

Therefore, the average salary for all 21 years is $\dfrac{(\$31,000 + \$71,000)}{2} = \$51,000$.

4. **(D):** Statement (1) states that there is an even number of consecutive integers. This statement tells you nothing about the actual values of the integers, but the average of an even number of consecutive integers will never be an integer. Therefore, the average of the *n* consecutive integers cannot equal 1. SUFFICIENT.

Statement (2) tells you that the sum of the *n* consecutive integers is positive, but smaller than *n*. Perhaps the most straightforward way to interpret this statement is to express it in terms of the average of the *n* numbers, rather than the sum. Average = Sum ÷ Number, so you can reinterpret the statement by dividing the compound inequality by *n*:

$$0 < S < n \qquad\qquad \frac{0}{n} < \frac{S}{n} < \frac{n}{n} \qquad\qquad 0 < \frac{S}{n} < 1$$

This tells you that the average integer in set S is larger than 0 but less than 1. Therefore, the average number in the set does NOT equal 1. SUFFICIENT. The correct answer is (D).

As a footnote, this situation can happen ONLY when there is an even number of integers, and when the "middle numbers" in the set are 0 and 1. For example, the set of consecutive integers {0, 1} has a median number of 0.5. Similarly, the set of consecutive integers {−3, −2, −1, 0, 1, 2, 3, 4} has a median number of 0.5.

5. **(B) 240:** First, determine the prime factorization of the product:

$7 \times 6 \times 5 \times 4 \times 3 = 7 \times (3 \times 2) \times 5 \times (2 \times 2) \times 3 = 2^3 \times 3^2 \times 5 \times 7$.

Next, write the prime factorization of each answer choice and determine which choice has a prime factor that is NOT in the prime factorization of the product above. Note that you can reuse a lot of your work, because the answer choices share many common prime factors:

(A):　　$120 = 10 \times 12 = 2^3 \times 3 \times 5$. All of these primes are in the factorization of $7 \times 6 \times 5 \times 4 \times 3$.

(B):　　$240 = 10 \times 24 = 2^4 \times 3 \times 5$. There is an extra 2 in this factorization that is NOT part of the factorization of $7 \times 6 \times 5 \times 4 \times 3$. Therefore, the product is not divisible by 240.

(C):　　$360 = 10 \times 36 = 2^3 \times 3^2 \times 5$. All of these primes are in the factorization of $7 \times 6 \times 5 \times 4 \times 3$.

(D):　　$840 = 10 \times 12 \times 7 = 2^3 \times 3 \times 5 \times 7$. All of these primes are in the factorization of $7 \times 6 \times 5 \times 4 \times 3$.

(E):　　$1,260 = 10 \times 18 \times 7 = 2^2 \times 3^2 \times 5 \times 7$. All of these primes are in the factorization of $7 \times 6 \times 5 \times 4 \times 3$.

An alternative method is to recognize that $120 = 5!$, which is a factor of the product of any 5 consecutive integers. Thus, answer choice (A) can be eliminated. Going further, you can rearrange $7 \times 6 \times 5 \times 4 \times 3$ as the product $7 \times 3 \times 2 \times 5 \times 4 \times 3$, which in turn can be rewritten as $7 \times 3 \times 5!$. Since $240 = 2 \times 5!$, you can now observe that $(7 \times 3 \times 5!) \div (2 \times 5!) = 21 \div 2$, which is not an integer. This tells you that (B) is the right answer.

6. **(C):** Statement (1) tells you that the largest (last) element in S is 55. However, you do not know how many elements are in S, or what the smallest (first) number in S is, so you cannot determine the average. For example, if the smallest number is 53, then the average is $(53 + 55) \div 2 = 54$. If the smallest number is 11, then the average is $(11 + 55) \div 2 = 33$. INSUFFICIENT.

Statement (2) tells you that there are 11 elements in the set. However, you know nothing about the size of the numbers in S. For example, if S is the set of integers from 1 to 11, the average is $(1 + 11) \div 2 = 6$. If S is the set of integers from 35 to 45, the average is $(35 + 45) \div 2 = 40$. INSUFFICIENT.

Combining Statements (1) and (2), you know that 55 is the largest element in S and there are 11 elements in S. Using the formula for the number of terms in a set of consecutive integers, you can find the smallest number in the set:

$$\text{Number of terms} = (\text{Last} - \text{First}) + 1$$
$$11 = (55 - \text{First}) + 1$$
$$\text{First} = 55 + 1 - 11 = 45$$

Therefore, Set S is the set of consecutive integers from 45 to 55. The average of the elements in S is $(45 + 55) \div 2 = 50$, and there are 11 elements. The sum of the elements is $50(11) = 550$. SUFFICIENT.

The correct answer is (C). Note that you did not need to compute this sum, because you knew three required pieces of information: (1) the last number in the series, which is 55; (2) the increment, which is 1; and (3) the number of terms, which is 11. As mentioned in the text, these three pieces of information fully define ANY evenly spaced set.

P

Appendix A

of

Word Problems

Official Guide Problem Sets

In This Chapter...

Official Guide Problem Sets

Problem Solving Set

Data Sufficiency Set

Official Guide Problem Sets

Now that you have completed *Word Problems*, it is time to test your skills on problems that have actually appeared on real GMAT exams over the past several years.

The problem sets that follow are composed of questions from two books published by the Graduate Management Admission Council® (the organization that develops the official GMAT exam):

> *The Official Guide for GMAT Review, 13th Edition*
> *The Official Guide for GMAT Quantitative Review, 2nd Edition*

These books contain quantitative questions that have appeared on past official GMAT exams. (The questions contained therein are the property of The Graduate Management Admission Council, which is not affiliated in any way with Manhattan GMAT.)

Although the questions in *The Official Guides* have been "retired" (they will not appear on future official GMAT exams), they are great practice questions.

In order to help you practice effectively, we have categorized every problem in *The Official Guides* by topic and subtopic. On the following pages, you will find two categorized lists:

1. **Problem Solving:**　Lists Problem Solving Word Problems questions contained in *The Official Guides* and categorizes them by subtopic.

2. **Data Sufficiency:**　Lists Data Sufficiency Word Problems questions contained in *The Official Guides* and categorizes them by subtopic.

Books 1 through 8 of Manhattan GMAT's Strategy Guide series each contain a unique *Official Guide* list that pertains to the specific topic of that particular book. If you complete all the practice problems contained on the *Official Guide* lists in each of these 8 Manhattan GMAT Strategy Guide books, you will have completed every single question published in *The Official Guides*.

Problem Solving Set

This set is from *The Official Guide for GMAT Review, 13th Edition* (pages 20–23 & 152–185), and *The Official Guide for GMAT Quantitative Review, 2nd Edition* (pages 62–86).

Solve each of the following problems in a notebook, making sure to demonstrate how you arrived at each answer by showing all of your work and computations. If you get stuck on a problem, look back at the Word Problems strategies and content contained in this guide to assist you.

Note: Problem numbers preceded by "D" refer to questions in the Diagnostic Test chapter of *The Official Guide for GMAT Review, 13th Edition* (pages 20–23).

Algebraic Translations:

13th Edition: 1, 4, 29, 60, 64, 76, 83, 88, 89, 93, 131, 137, 140, 153, 154, 167, 184, 203, 205
Quantitative Review: 3, 13, 19, 25, 51, 52, 54, 62, 75, 94, 115, 124, 126, 127, 171

Rates & Work:

13th Edition: 23, 34, 38, 49, 79, 81, 86, 103, 139, 162, 168, 207, D24
Quantitative Review: 16, 22, 23, 37, 87, 90, 119, 130, 136, 140, 142, 173

Statistics:

13th Edition: 12, 16, 30, 53, 91, 101, 109, 112, 119, 132, 145, 183, 208, D9
Quantitative Review: 32, 63, 70, 81, 84, 104, 116, 129, 137, 148, 161

Consecutive Integers:

13th Edition: 67, 90, 124, 158, 172, 221, 225, D2
Quantitative Review: 11

Overlapping Sets:

13th Edition: 25, 136, 178, 186, 189, 222, D14, D4, D6
Quantitative Review: 18, 64, 146

Extra Problem Types:

13th Edition: 33, 39
Quantitative Review: 56, 80, 110, 168

Data Sufficiency Set

This set is from *The Official Guide for GMAT Review, 13th Edition* (pages 24–26 & 274–291), and *The Official Guide for GMAT Quantitative Review, 2nd Edition* (pages 152–163).

Solve each of the following problems in a notebook, making sure to demonstrate how you arrived at each answer by showing all of your work and computations. If you get stuck on a problem, look back at the Word Problems strategies and content contained in this guide to assist you.

Practice **rephrasing** both the questions and the statements. The majority of data sufficiency problems can be rephrased; however, if you have difficulty rephrasing a problem, try testing numbers to solve it. It is especially important that you familiarize yourself with the directions for data sufficiency problems, and that you memorize the 5 fixed answer choices that accompany all data sufficiency problems.

Note: Problem numbers preceded by "D" refer to questions in the Diagnostic Test chapter of *The Official Guide for GMAT Review, 13th Edition* (pages 24–26).

Algebraic Translations:

13th Edition: 9, 28, 44, 54, 57, 59, 65, 71, 78, 124, 126, 132, 141, 142, 147, 153, 158, 174, D27
Quantitative Review: 6, 7, 9, 12, 13, 17, 26, 27, 29, 33, 84, 97, 108

Rates & Work:

13th Edition: 12, 16, 22, 68, 90, 106, 107, 108, 115
Quantitative Review: 38, 47, 55, 71, 117

Statistics:

13th Edition: 20, 37, 38, 70, 77, 84, 87, 95, 105, 109, 110, 120, 121, 123, 139, 143, 144, 146, 154, D31, D32, D43, D46
Quantitative Review: 1, 14, 34, 41, 66, 74, 101, 103, 112, 118

Consecutive Integers:

13th Edition: 18, 64, 112
Quantitative Review: 20, 86

Overlapping Sets:

13th Edition: 5, 21, 34, 49, 66, 93, 134, 137, 138, D29, D34, D47
Quantitative Review: 10, 63, 85, 116

Extra Problem Types:

13th Edition: 6, 45, 89, 103, 140, D45
Quantitative Review: 8